NEW DIRECTIONS FOR ADULT AND CONTINUING EDUCATION

Ralph G. Brockett, *University of Tennessee, Knoxville*
EDITOR-IN-CHIEF

Alan B. Knox, *University of Wisconsin, Madison*
CONSULTING EDITOR

# Confronting Racism and Sexism

Elisabeth Hayes
*University of Wisconsin, Madison*

Scipio A. J. Colin III
*North Carolina State University, Raleigh*

EDITORS

Number 61, Spring 1994

JOSSEY-BASS PUBLISHERS
San Francisco

JUN 28 1994

CONFRONTING RACISM AND SEXISM
*Elisabeth Hayes, Scipio A. J. Colin III* (eds.)
New Directions for Adult and Continuing Education, n
*Ralph G. Brockett*, Editor-in-Chief
*Alan B. Knox*, Consulting Editor

Microfilm copies of issues and articles are available in 16mm and 35mm, as well as microfiche in 105mm, through University Microfilms Inc., 300 North Zeeb Road, Ann Arbor, Michigan 48106-1346.

LC 85-644750          ISSN 0195-2242          ISBN 1-55542-717-0

NEW DIRECTIONS FOR ADULT AND CONTINUING EDUCATION is part of The Jossey-Bass Higher and Adult Education Series and is published quarterly by Jossey-Bass Inc., Publishers, 350 Sansome Street, San Francisco, California 94104-1342 (publication number USPS 493-930). Second-class postage paid at San Francisco, California, and at additional mailing offices. POSTMASTER: Send address changes to New Directions for Adult and Continuing Education, Jossey-Bass Inc., Publishers, 350 Sansome Street, San Francisco, California 94104-1342.

SUBSCRIPTIONS for 1994 cost $47.00 for individuals and $62.00 for institutions, agencies, and libraries.

EDITORIAL CORRESPONDENCE should be sent to the Editor-in-Chief, Ralph G. Brockett, Department of Educational Leadership, University of Tennessee, 239 Claxton Addition, Knoxville, Tennessee 37996-3400.

Cover photograph by Wernher Krutein/PHOTOVAULT © 1990.

Epigraph in Chapter Seven from Jenny Yamato, "Something about the Subject Makes It Hard to Name." In CHANGING OUR POWER: An Introduction to Woman's Studies edited by Cochran et al. Copyright 1987 by Kendall/Hunt Publishing Co. Used with permission.

Epigraph in Chapter One reprinted with permission of Charles Scribner's Sons, an imprint of Macmillan Publishing Company from TWO NATIONS: BLACK AND WHITE, SEPARATE, HOSTILE, UNEQUAL by Andrew Hacker. Copyright © 1992 Andrew Hacker.

Manufactured in the United States of America. Nearly all Jossey-Bass books, jackets, and periodicals are printed on recycled paper that contains at least 50 percent recycled waste, including 10 percent postconsumer waste. Many of our materials are also printed with vegetable-based inks; during the printing process, these inks emit fewer volatile organic compounds (VOCs) than petroleum-based inks. VOCs contribute to the formation of smog.

# CONTENTS

# Editors' Notes

Racism and sexism are enduring social problems in all aspects of our society, ranging from the dynamics of individual interactions to the policies and procedures of our dominant sociocultural institutions. The lives of people of color and women continue to be affected negatively by racist and sexist attitudes, ideologies, and practices. The longevity of these problems and the damage wrought in the lives of these individuals make this volume, *Confronting Racism and Sexism*, not only warranted but long overdue.

Educational institutions and practices have a major role in the perpetuation of racism and sexism. Curiously, there is very little literature on the dynamics of racism and sexism in the context of adult and continuing education. It is beyond the scope of these notes to address the reasons for this fact, which emphasizes that we must devote increased attention to the racism and sexism in our field. Otherwise, we may believe that adult education is somehow immune from or not responsible for the injustices that plague our society. We believe that racism and sexism continue to perpetuate inequities in adult education and that they can be found in every aspect of our practice, ranging from classroom instruction to the activities of professional associations, and that they can also be found in the concepts and theories that constitute our knowledge base. We readily acknowledge that the task of identifying and changing racist and sexist beliefs and practices is not an easy one. However, if we wish our educational programs and professional interactions to be truly inclusive and if we wish to educate others to work equitably and effectively with the members of diverse populations, we must confront and challenge racist and sexist assumptions.

As editors, we dealt with a variety of issues as we clarified the focus of this sourcebook. The need to limit the scope of the volume led us to make omissions that some readers might question. Our first decision was to deal not with diversity in some broad and general sense but with particular "isms." This decision reflects a philosophical and political stance as much as it reflects the material need to limit the book's content. We wished to deal directly with issues of prejudice, power, and privilege that a general discussion of cultural diversity or inclusive approaches to education might have the effect of minimizing. Our second decision was to focus on racism and sexism and exclude other forms of discrimination and prejudice, such as homophobia or ageism. This decision was based on our recognition that we could not deal adequately with all isms in a single volume. We openly acknowledge that our choice of racism and sexism reflects our own particular priorities.

Nevertheless, even this relatively limited focus prevents us from addressing many issues. One is the impact of class on individual experiences of racism and sexism. The issue of class is related to the broad challenge of clarifying the complex ways in which multiple forms of oppression overlap and intersect. We and the other authors have tried to acknowledge such intersections, most notably in the experience of African Ameripean women.[1] However, we also considered it necessary to make generalizations about the experiences of women and people of color in order to demonstrate the systematic inequities known collectively as *racism* and *sexism*. Despite these limitations, we hope that this book will serve as a starting point for further consideration of racism and sexism as well as other forms of oppression in the context of adult education.

The purpose of this volume is to enable adult and continuing educators to recognize the existence and consequences of racism and sexism in their own practice. Just as important, the chapters in this volume provide explanations, examples, and techniques that can help and encourage readers to begin to change racist and sexist practices.

In Chapter One, we set the stage by discussing some conceptual issues related to the definition of racism and sexism. Since the current effects of racism and sexism are often unacknowledged or minimized, we describe the considerable disadvantages that women and people of color still experience in two areas—employment and education—and the factors that perpetuate these disadvantages.

The power and longevity of racism and sexism are due in part to their basis in implicit and explicit beliefs and values. Daniele D. Flannery, in Chapter Two, identifies racist and sexist biases in current theories of adult learning and in our assumptions about theory building and describes their role in racist and sexist practices. She describes strategies that all adult educators can use to create new and more inclusive perspectives on adult learners.

How to overcome racism and sexism in classroom teaching situations is a concern that many educators share. In Chapter Three, Vanessa Sheared introduces us to an instructional approach based on an Africentric feminist or womanist epistemological framework.[2] This approach is intended to give voice to individuals and groups whom traditional methods of instruction have silenced. Sheared describes the significance of the multiple and "polyrhythmic realities" of instructor and students in shaping the learning environment. She describes a process that adult educators can use to acknowledge and value learners' diverse experiences and their differing ways of understanding and knowing.

In Chapter Four, Donna D. Amstutz reviews strategies for staff development that can be used to help adult educators in any setting recognize and overcome racism and sexism in their own practice. The chapter identifies both formal and informal staff development activities that emphasize a process for individual growth and development of more equitable beliefs and behaviors.

In Chapter Five, Scipio A. J. Colin III raises our awareness of other types of bias through a discussion of racism in adult education graduate programs.

She describes how racism is manifest in the recruitment and retention of faculty and students and in curriculum content. The chapter concludes with policy and programmatic recommendations and a selected bibliography of Africentric resources.

Racism and sexism in our knowledge base, curricula, teaching methods, and other practices are integrally related to inequitable power relationships in the professionalization of adult education. In Chapter Six, Juanita Johnson Bailey, Elizabeth J. Tisdell, and Ronald M. Cervero describe the nature of professionalization in adult education and focus on racism and sexism in the professional training of adult educators in higher education. They suggest ways in which both faculty and students can make confronting inequities in higher education a starting point for challenging racism and sexism in the professionalization of adult education more broadly.

In the final chapter, Elisabeth Hayes summarizes key themes and strategies that individuals can use to overcome biases in their own beliefs and practice as adult educators. She also describes ways in which individuals can work with others to create broad changes in institutional practices and in professional associations through their teaching.

Elisabeth Hayes
Scipio A. J. Colin III
Editors

## Notes

1. The term *African Ameripean* is used here and in chapters 1 and 5 because of the authors' belief that terms such as *colored, black, Negro, Afro-American,* and *African American* are culturally inappropriate and historically incorrect. Any term that is used to identify a race of people also identifies a land of origin and should be genetically, socioculturally, and historically correct. *African-Ameripean* describes any person of African descent born in America. The use of *African* denotes the primary genetic roots and land of origin (there is no "Afrocan" continent). *Ameri-* reflects the voluntary assimilation with various Native American tribal societies (particularly Cherokee and Seminole) and *-pean* reflects the forced assimilation with various European ethnic groups, particularly the British, French, and Irish, during the period of slavery in the United States.

2. The terms *Africentric* and *Africentrism* are intentionally used by the authors of chapters 3 and 5 rather than the more common *Afrocentric* and *Afrocentrism*. Africentrism is a sociocultural and philosophical perspective that reflects the intellectual traditions of both a culture and a continent. It is grounded in these seven basic values (the Swahili term is provided first, followed by its English translation): Umoja (unity), Kujichagulia (self-determination), Ujima (collective work and responsibility), Ujamaa (cooperative economics), Nia (purpose), Kuumba (creativity), and Imani (faith). In contrast, Afrocentrism is considered by these authors to represent an integrationist perspective that incorporates elements of European traditions. The term *Africentrism* was originally used by Colin (1988).

**Reference**

Colin, S.A.J, III. "Voices from Beyond the Veil: Marcus Garvey, the Universal Negro Improvement Association, and the Education of African Ameripean Adults." Unpublished doctoral dissertation, Northern Illinois University, 1988.

*ELISABETH HAYES is associate professor of continuing and vocational education at the University of Wisconsin–Madison.*

*SCIPIO A. J. COLIN III is assistant professor of adult and continuing education at North Carolina State University, Raleigh.*

*What is the nature of racism and sexism in society today?*

# Racism and Sexism in the United States: Fundamental Issues

*Elisabeth Hayes, Scipio A. J. Colin III*

> Ideas about equality and inferiority and superiority are not simply
> figments in people's minds. Such sentiments have an impact on how
> institutions operate, and opinions tend to be self-fulfilling
> —A. Hacker (1992, p. 29)

Racism and sexism are societal problems that affect all social institutions and human interactions. They are manifest at a variety of levels ranging from individual beliefs and behaviors to the values and practices supported by institutions and societies. Despite recent assertions that racism and sexism are problems of the past, their impact today is still significant, although it may have become more difficult to identify.

To understand racism and sexism in adult education, we must consider their dynamics and effects in today's society as a whole. In this chapter, we discuss the nature of racism and sexism, current evidence of their impact on women and people of color in employment and education, and the ways in which individual behaviors, educational institutions, and organizational practices perpetuate them. It is important to note that racism and sexism are not the same thing, and there are important differences in their origins and consequences that we cannot address at length in this chapter. In general, this chapter must be considered an introduction to some complicated and controversial issues. We hope that readers will use it as a stepping-stone to further reading and reflection.

New Directions for Adult and Continuing Education, no. 61, Spring 1994 © Jossey-Bass Publishers

## Defining Racism and Sexism

Some of the issues surrounding racism and sexism concern the way in which these terms should be defined. Kramarae and Treichler (1985, p. 411) offer a definition of sexism that is particularly useful as a starting point: "behavior, policy, language, or other action of men or women which expresses the institutionalized, systematic, comprehensive, or consistent view that women are inferior." Colin and Preciphs (1991, p. 62) express a similar perspective when they define racism as "conscious or unconscious, and expressed in actions or attitudes initiated by individuals, groups, or institutions that treat human beings unjustly because of their skin pigmentation. Therefore, racism is expressed in attitudes, behaviors, and institutions."

These definitions suggest at least two aspects of racism and sexism that are particularly important. First, racism and sexism are part of the fabric of our society; they are reflected not only in individual actions but also in our institutions and even in the language that we use to understand and describe our world. For their perpetrators, racist and sexist actions are not always easy to identify, nor are their effects always obvious. Many instances of racism and sexism may seem relatively harmless when they are considered in isolation. Frye (1983) uses the concept of oppression to describe the impact of the pervasive, systematic, and often invisible barriers that sexism creates. Her arguments can be applied to racism. She suggests that the metaphor of a bird cage can help us to understand why oppression can be so hard to see and recognize. If you look at only one wire of the cage, it is hard to imagine how it could act as an effective restraint on a bird's behavior. Only when you see the network of systematically related wires can you understand the confining power of the cage. It is essential to become aware of the multiple and reinforcing manifestations of racism and sexism to appreciate the impact that they have on the freedom and opportunities of individuals.

Second, racism and sexism reflect belief systems that, by explicitly or implicitly portraying people of color and women as deficient, justify discriminatory treatment. These belief systems or race and gender ideologies serve as a means of social control and maintain the power of the dominant group (Chafe, 1992). Race and gender are inherently social concepts. Our beliefs about differences between women and men or between various racial groups are shaped by historical, social, and political factors (Omi and Winant, 1992). We typically consider these differences to be biological or "natural," and we use them to define appropriate roles and behavior for groups of people. However, these beliefs in fact reflect stereotypes that perpetuate inaccurate generalizations about people's characteristics. These stereotypes are reflected in current widespread notions; for example, women are innately more nurturing and empathic than men, and African Ameripeans are more violent than Euro-Americans.[1] In our society, the media play a major role both in the creation and in the maintenance of stereotypes, and recent films and television shows have been criticized for promoting images of African Ameripeans as criminals and drug addicts (Wilkerson, 1993).

There is some controversy over the question of who can be the object of racism and sexism. Rothenberg (1992) makes a distinction between prejudice on the one hand and racism and sexism on the other. She defines *prejudice* as an individual's negative feelings about other people based on certain characteristics. In contrast, racism and sexism involve prejudice plus power, that is, prejudice that is reflected in and reinforced by broader social institutions and dominant ideology. From this perspective, men cannot be the objects of sexism, nor can white people be the object of racism. The authors of the chapters in the volume have adopted this viewpoint. Thus, in this chapter, we discuss sexism as the subordination of women and racism as the subordination of people of color. Moreover, we focus on the experience of African Ameripeans in our discussion of racism. While other people of color clearly suffer the effects of racism, racism in the United States has the most negative consequences for African Ameripeans (Hacker, 1992).

Attention to the intersection of racism and sexism in the experience of women of color is very recent. While data analyzed by both race and gender are very limited (Ries and Stone, 1992), it is evident that patterns of disadvantage for women of color are both different and often more severe. For example, African Ameripean women have lower average earnings than white women and men of either race (Ries and Stone, 1992). There is evidence that African Ameripean women are twice as likely to experience sexual harassment as white women (Benokraitis and Feagin, 1986). Moreover, the stereotypes about African Ameripean women have differed from the stereotypes about white women. The stereotypes about African Ameripean women have been used to blame them for the general economic and social disadvantages of their race. One such stereotype is that of the assertive, aggressive black matriarch who intimidates or dominates men and otherwise does not conform to the roles appropriate to the female gender. This stereotype has been held responsible for problems ranging from male unemployment to the breakdown in "normal" family structures and the tendency of African Ameripean children to fail in school (Collins, 1990). Wherever possible in this chapter, we have pointed out the unique situation of African Ameripean women. Increasing our understanding of the diverse experiences of racism and sexism is an essential component of the future agenda for change.

Racism and sexism have been challenged repeatedly over the course of history. Since the 1960s, the civil rights and women's movements have been successful in raising general awareness of discrimination against women and people of color, in stimulating a variety of policies and practices intended to overcome this discrimination, and in creating some notable changes in their social roles and opportunities. The mass media have dramatized the achievements of exceptional women and people of color and thereby created the impression that racism and sexism now offer few if any barriers to wealth, power, and recognition. Nevertheless, there is considerable evidence that the opportunities and status of women and people of color have not improved as significantly or consistently as commonly believed. In general, progress toward the reduction of gender and race-related inequities in some areas has been matched by the lack of progress and even negative trends in others. In the next sections, we focus on the disadvantages that African Ameripeans and women still experience in the areas of employment and education.

## Economic Impact of Racism and Sexism: Income and Occupations

Economic disadvantage is one obvious indicator of the effects of racism and sexism. Women, particularly those who are heads of households, and African Ameripeans are considerably more likely to experience poverty than white men. About one in three African Ameripeans lives in poverty, compared to about one in ten whites. For African Ameripean female heads of households, the ratio increases to one in two (Mantsios, 1992). In 1991, African Ameripeans had an unemployment rate of 12.4 percent, more than twice the rate of 6.0 percent for Euro-Americans (United States Bureau of the Census, 1992). The unemployment rates for women of both races were slightly lower than those for men of the same race. In fact, the number of women in the paid work force reached an all-time high of 58 percent in 1990 (Ries and Stone, 1992). However, women are more likely than men to be employed part-time or in seasonal or temporary jobs (Pearce, 1993). Other major causes of economic inequities are persistent pay differentials and occupational stratification.

**Pay Differentials.** In 1989, the median earnings for African Ameripean men employed full-time were $20,426, only 71.5 percent of the $28,541 recorded for white men. Women on the whole earned less than men of either race. White women were paid $18,922 (66.2 percent of white male earnings), and African Ameripean women earned $17,389, only 60.9 percent of white male earnings (National Committee on Pay Equity, 1992).

Trend data indicate that the wage differential between white and African Ameripean men has decreased only slightly since 1980, when the earnings of African Ameripean men were 70.7 percent of white men's earnings (National Committee on Pay Equity, 1992). While the overall ratio of female-to-male earnings represents an improvement from the 60 percent noted in 1980, the current ratio is roughly comparable to the female-male wage ratio in the mid 1950s. The "increase" really represents the regaining of ground lost in the 1960s and 1970s (Rhode, 1993). Moreover, the narrowing of this earnings gap can be attributed in part to a decline in men's wages, not to increased wages for women, which suggests that women's actual economic gains in the last decade were small.

The National Committee on Pay Equity (1992) reports that a considerable proportion of the earnings differentials cannot be explained by differences in education, labor force experience, or years in the labor force. According to one study that it cites, these factors typically accounted for less than 25 percent and never for more than half of the wage gaps observed, a fact suggesting that there are significant race and gender biases.

**Occupational Segregation.** A considerable proportion of the inequity in wages can be attributed to occupational segregation. A number of studies have indicated that median earnings decrease as the percentage of women and people of color in an occupation increases (National Committee on Pay Equity, 1992). Despite efforts to recruit women into nontraditional occupations, about half of women in the paid labor force are employed in occupations that are at least 80 percent female (Rhode, 1993). As Rhode (1993, p. 253) wryly observes, "While men and women are now entitled to equal pay for the same work, relatively few males and few females have performed the same work." The so-called growth areas of employment over the last decades consist primarily of low-paying jobs like clerical, retail, and service positions, and these are precisely the kinds of jobs that women entering the work force are taking: More than nine of every ten women added to U.S. payrolls in last three decades—a total 39 million women—worked in the service sector (Ries and Stone, 1992). Occupations are further segregated by race, with women of color overrepresented in low-skill, low-paid jobs, such as health aide and private household worker. Jobs that had the highest concentration of black men include stevedore, garbage collector, longshore equipment operator, and baggage porter (National Committee on Pay Equity, 1992; Ries and Stone, 1992).

The most visible progress toward increased occupational integration for women can be found in their entry into certain male-dominated professions, such as law, medicine, and management. However, in 1990 women comprised only 20.8 percent of the lawyers and judges, 19.3 percent of the physicians, and 9.5 percent of the dentists (National Committee on Pay Equity, 1992). Progress toward the integration of women in blue-collar occupations also has been limited. Overall, women hold only about 20 percent of the jobs in the skilled trades. In certain specialties, there has been virtually no integration. There have even been some declines, as in carpentry, where the percentage of women dropped during the 1980s from 1.7 to 1.3 (Pearce, 1993). Moreover, there is little evidence that male representation in traditionally female-dominated occupations is increasing. For example, 99 percent of the secretaries still are women (Ries and Stone, 1992).

## Racism, Sexism, and Educational Outcomes

The formal educational system in our society has an instrumental role in controlling access to higher-paying occupations, knowledge, power, and status. The success of women and people of color relative to white men in the educational system offers another indication of the persistent effects of racism and sexism. Since the 1960s, a number of strategies have been used to promote equity for women and people of color at all levels of education. While these strategies have had some positive effects, particularly for white women, there continue to be significant disparities in educational achievement. Moreover, the occupational benefits that women and African Ameripeans enjoy for comparable levels of educational attainment are still inferior to those enjoyed by white males.

**Educational Achievement.** Some indicators suggest that women now experience comparable or greater educational success than men. Women earn better grades than their male counterparts throughout their educational careers (Ries and Stone, 1992). There now appear to be few real differences in female and male performance on most tests of reading and mathematic abilities, and gender differences have declined significantly over the last twenty years (Bailey and others, 1993). In contrast, gaps in academic skill proficiency between African Ameripeans and whites are considerable, although some of the gaps have narrowed. For example, in 1971 the differences in National Assessment of Educational Progress (NAEP) reading and math scores between African Ameripean and white seventeen-year-olds were about twice as great as the differences recorded in 1990 (National Center for Education Statistics, 1992).

Both college-bound women and African Ameripeans continue to score lower than white men on the Scholastic Aptitude Test (SAT), which serves as an important criterion for college admissions. In 1992, women scored about ten points lower than men on the SAT verbal test and about forty-five points lower on the SAT math test. These differences have remained virtually unchanged since 1976. African Ameripean students do much less well than white students, although their relative performance has improved somewhat. On the average, in 1992 African Ameripeans scored 91 points lower than whites on the SAT verbal test and 106 points lower on the SAT math test. In 1976, the difference was 119 points on the verbal and 139 points on the math test. Explanations for the continued gender and race-related discrepancies range from test bias to a tendency among women and African Ameripeans to take less rigorous math courses (De Witt, 1993; National Center for Education Statistics, 1992).

Since 1989, women in general have been earning the majority of degrees at all levels with the exception of the doctorate (Ries and Stone, 1992). Degree attainment is considerably lower for African Ameripeans than it is for whites. In 1990, about 78 percent of African Ameripean nineteen- and twenty-year-olds had completed high school, compared to about 83 percent for whites in the same age group. Girls of both races are less likely to drop out than boys of the same race. African Ameripean high school graduates are also less likely than whites both to go to college and to earn college degrees. In 1991, about 14 percent of the African Ameripean high school graduates between the ages of twenty-five and twenty-nine had completed four years of college, compared to 30 percent of the whites (National Center for Education Statistics, 1992).

There are considerable differences in the fields of study that women and men of different racial groups choose, although the differences have become smaller in some fields. Women are earning a growing proportion of professional degrees. For example, in 1989 women earned 33 percent of all medical degrees and 41 percent of all law degrees. However, white men continue to dominate fields that typically lead to occupations with higher salaries and prestige, such as the physical sciences. In 1989, women still earned only 15 percent of all the bachelor's degrees awarded in engineering (Ries and Stone, 1992). Black men are also less likely than white men to major in fields like computer science and engineering and more likely than white men to choose technical/professional areas, such as health sciences and communications. Women in general are three times more likely than men to major in education (National Center for Education Statistics, 1992).

The differences are the most pronounced at the level of the highest degrees. For example, in 1990 almost 56 percent of the doctorates earned by African Ameripean women were in education, compared to 30 percent for white women, 33 percent for African Ameripean men, and only 15 percent for white men. In contrast, about 27 percent of the doctorates earned by white men were in the natural sciences, compared to 9 percent for African Ameripean men, 16 percent for white women, and 5 percent for African Ameripean women (National Center for Education Statistics, 1992).

**Education and Occupational Outcomes.** The economic returns for education are significantly different for women and African Ameripeans. Among full-time workers in 1991, the median annual income for college graduates between the ages of twenty-five and thirty-four was $35,484 for white men, $28,299 for African Ameripean men, $27,287 for white women, and $22,959 for African Ameripean women (National Center for Education Statistics, 1992). A longitudinal study of high school graduates from 1972 indicated that women's earnings were less than men's even when other factors, such as having children and job experience, were controlled for (Adelman, 1991).

It is possible to explain some of these differences by the occupations chosen by women and men of different racial groups. In 1986, education majors had the lowest starting salaries (18 percent below average), while starting salaries for computer science and engineering majors were 36 percent above the average (National Center for Education Statistics, 1992).

Other differences can be explained by race and gender-related segregation within occupations. For example, Higginbotham and Cannon (1988) observed that many African Ameripean professionals work in public sector jobs in segregated settings serving primarily other people of color and earning relatively low salaries. The recent entry of women into the professions does not entirely explain the disproportionately small number of women who have reached positions of power and status in such areas as management, law, and higher education.

## The Perpetuation of Racism and Sexism

In the past, overt race and sex discrimination was not only socially acceptable, it was required by governmental legislation. Today, legislation and other social sanctions work against such discrimination: "White and male supremacy are no longer popularly accepted American values" (United States Commission on Civil Rights, 1992, p. 10). Nevertheless, it is unrealistic to expect that the concerted efforts of many groups and individuals could eradicate deeply ingrained societal beliefs and practices within a few decades. Just as racism and sexism exist at many levels, there are barriers to change at many levels. Benokraitis and Feagin (1986) suggest that, while legislation has reduced overt discrimination, more subtle and covert discrimination remains quite prevalent. Pervasive stereotypes, bolstered by an ideology that justifies and maintains the power and privilege of a white male elite, continue to support racism and sexism. This ideology argues that racism and sexism no longer exist and that the purported "victims" of racism and sexism—women and people of color—are to blame for any apparent disadvantages that they experience.

Individual beliefs and behavior reflect these stereotypes and this ideology. They often cause unconscious discrimination. Even more perniciously, they affect the self-perceptions and choices of women and people of color. Educational institutions serve as a powerful mechanism for perpetuating sexist and racist beliefs as well as for shaping individual behavior in ways that conform to existing stereotypes. Seemingly "neutral" practices and policies in the workplace and other institutions remain biased and perpetuate white male privilege (Benokraitis and Feagin, 1986; Rhode, 1993).

**Individual Beliefs and Behavior.** At one level, racism and sexism are manifest in the prejudiced attitudes and actions of individuals. The effects of racism and sexism can also be seen in the self-perceptions and aspirations of women and people of color.

*Individual Discrimination.* Discrimination against women and people of color can be both obvious and subtle, intentional and unintentional. More blatant examples of individual discrimination include sexual harassment, physical violence, and racist or sexist jokes. Even people who do not hold conscious prejudices can engage in subtle sexist and racist behaviors. For example, the comments of women in formal meetings or informal discussions can be ignored because of unconscious assumptions that their ideas are less valuable than those of men. Research has shown that evaluators tend to rate identical resumes or scholarly articles significantly lower if the applicant or author is identified as a woman (Rhode, 1993).

Unintentional discrimination may be particularly hard to recognize because it can be motivated by a genuine desire to treat women or people of color in a helpful manner. For example, unconscious assumptions about their abilities can lead school counselors to discourage women or people of color from taking more challenging courses or subjects and thus reduce their potential for entering jobs with increased status and wages. Assumptions that domestic responsibilities take precedence over professional development may lead educators to exclude adult women students from opportunities to participate in informal learning activities.

*Individual Choices and Self-Perceptions.* Women and people of color are not immune to the influence of stereotypes or sexist and racist ideology. They are socialized to accept stereotypes. This process can lead them to make choices that put them at a disadvantage in the workplace and in other arenas. Accepting stereotypes can mean that they believe themselves to be inadequate or inferior, that they lower their aspirations, and even that they accept overtly discriminatory treatment. The absence of female or African Ameripean role models may make certain occupations or life-styles seem unattainable or inappropriate. Awareness of the potential costs may limit the extent to which an individual will challenge the status quo. For example, women may deliberately avoid male-dominated occupations, such as the skilled trades, because of the harassment that they anticipate from employers or coworkers. Faced with a choice between abandoning cultural values and community affiliations and pursuing higher education or professional mobility, people of color may reject education and advancement (Higginbotham and Cannon, 1988).

**Educational Institutions.** Educational institutions play a major role in the promotion of racist and sexist beliefs and conformity to stereotypical behavior. This process occurs through the formal and the informal curriculum at all levels (Bailey and others, 1993).

*The Formal Curriculum.* A host of studies has documented gender and racial biases in instructional materials. These biases include the use of racist and sexist language, omission of the contributions to history of women and minorities, the use of books written primarily by white males, and the portrayal of women and people of color in stereotypical roles. Over the last twenty years, the efforts of educators, authors, and publishers to create and use materials that portray women and people of color in more positive ways have reduced some of these biases. However, recent studies indicate that significant biases still exist in present-day curricula. For example, Bailey and others (1993) cite research from 1990 identifying ongoing language bias and omission and misrepresentation of women's perspectives and contributions to society in instructional materials designed to be used under current guidelines on gender and race equity. A 1989 study found that, of the ten books most often used in high school English courses, only one had been written by a woman, and none were by people of color (Bailey and others, 1993). Such biases have an impact on students' perceptions of women and people of color as well as on their own self-image and goals.

*The Informal Curriculum.* The dynamics of instructional activities also play a significant role in the shaping of students' beliefs and behavior. Racial and gender biases in teacher-student interactions at all levels of education have received particular attention. Bailey and others (1993) summarize research indicating that white male students have more extensive and favorable inter-actions with teachers than male students from other racial and ethnic minori-ties and than all female students. Teachers' perceptions of students' abilities also appear to vary with race and gender. For example, one study found that, when the achievement of black girls and white boys was comparable, teachers attributed the girls' success to hard work and assumed that the boys were not working up to their full potential. The differences observed in interactions and expectations may have an impact on students' academic achievement and motivation to succeed. They may also help to explain the drop in self-esteem that girls experience over the course of their education. This drop is particu-larly evident in the areas of math and science. At the highest degree levels, studies have shown that women's confidence in their academic ability declines, while men report that their confidence increases. It is particularly disturbing that this decline has no relationship to women's actual ability as indicated by grades (Bailey and others, 1993).

**Organizational Policies and Practices.** A number of common organiza-tional practices and policies, some that appear to be neutral and nondiscrimi-natory, continue to discriminate against women and people of color (United States Commission on Civil Rights, 1992). Some of these practices are biased because they reflect and favor a life situation that is more common and accessi-ble to white men than it is to members of other groups. For example, the typi-cally low wages, limited potential for advancement, and lack of fringe benefits for part-time workers discriminates against women, who constitute two-thirds of the part-time workers. Formal and informal sanctions against interruptions in careers have adverse effects for women, because they are more likely than men to take time off from their jobs to care for children and sick or aging relatives.

Other practices are discriminatory because of the lingering effects of past racism and sexism. For example, one study found that women sales clerks were consistently excluded from positions in retail departments and stores with opportunities for high commissions (Benokraitis and Feagin, 1986). The prac-tice of recruiting by word of mouth among networks of professional colleagues can be discriminatory if these networks consist primarily of white males. For jobs that white males have traditionally held, seniority rules can reduce job security for women and people of color hired recently and pose barriers to their promotion (United States Commission on Civil Rights, 1992). For exam-ple, increased competition and the resulting need to cut production costs led one General Electric plant to eliminate the jobs of women and people of color, who had only recently gained access to these positions (Kilborn, 1993). The work force remaining consisted almost entirely of white men, and there was little prospect for increased diversification or expansion in the next decade.

## Conclusion

Racism and sexism are societal problems that affect all human interactions and social institutions. Increased public awareness, government policies, and other efforts have reduced some of their negative consequences, but many still remain. We have noted some consequences in this chapter. Others, such as health issues and limited political power, could be added to the overall picture of disadvantage.

What can be done to address these issues? Our discussion recognizes that there have been some positive changes in the status of women and people of color. Nevertheless, a variety of strategies will be essential if these changes are to be maintained and inequities are to be further reduced. Adult education can be one powerful vehicle for confronting racist and sexist practices. For example, many employers are now using educational programs to raise their employees' awareness of racist and sexist attitudes and behaviors. However, adult educators may first need to recognize the biases in their own practice. The effects of racism and sexism are reflected in adult education, in patterns of learner participation and achievement, and in the professional preparation of adult educators themselves. Many adult educators remain unaware of the racism and sexism reflected in their individual actions, educational curricula, and teaching strategies as well as in the practices of their organizations. The chapters that follow explore these areas. We cannot address racism and sexism as societal problems until we are able to recognize that they exist in our own practice and we challenge them there.

## Note

1. Use of the term *African Ameripean* is discussed in the Editors' Notes.

## References

Adelman, C. *Women at Thirtysomething: Paradoxes of Attainment.* Washington, D.C.: Office of Educational Research and Improvement, U.S. Department of Education, 1991.

Bailey, S. M., Burbridge, L., Campbell, P., Jackson, B., Marx, F., and McIntosh, P. "Girls, Gender, and Schools: Excerpts from *The AAUW Report: How Schools Shortchange Girls.*" In S. Matteo (ed.), *American Women in the Nineties: Today's Critical Issues.* Boston: Northeastern University Press, 1993.

Benokraitis, N. V., and Feagin, J. R. *Modern Sexism: Blatant, Subtle, and Covert Discrimination.* Englewood Cliffs, N.J.: Prentice Hall, 1986.

Chafe, W. "Sex and Race: The Analogy of Social Control." In P. S. Rothenburg (ed.), *Race, Class, and Gender in the United States: An Integrated Study.* New York: St. Martin's Press, 1992.

Colin, S.A.J., III, and Preciphs, T. K. "Perceptual Patterns and the Learning Environment: Confronting White Racism." In R. Hiemstra (ed.), *Creating Environments for Effective Adult Learning.* New Directions for Adult and Continuing Education, no. 50. San Francisco: Jossey-Bass, 1991.

Collins, P. H. *Black Feminist Thought: Knowledge, Consciousness, and the Politics of Empowerment.* Boston: Unwin Hyman, 1990.

De Witt, K. "College Board Scores Are Up for Second Consecutive Year." *The New York Times,* Aug. 19, 1993, pp. A1, A8.

Frye, M. *The Politics of Reality: Essays in Feminist Theory.* Trumansburg, N.Y.: Crossing Press, 1983.

Hacker, A. *Two Nations.* New York: Charles Scribner's Sons, 1992.

Higginbotham, E., and Cannon, L. *Rethinking Mobility: Towards a Race and Gender Inclusive Theory.* Memphis, Tenn.: Center for Research on Women, Memphis State University, 1988.

Kilborn, P. T. "An American Workplace, After the Deluge." *The New York Times,* Sept. 5, 1993, Section 3, pp. 1, 4.

Kramarae, C., and Treichler, P. A. *A Feminist Dictionary*. London: Pandora Books, 1985.

Mantsios, G. "Rewards and Opportunities: The Politics and Economics of Class in the U.S." In P. S. Rothenburg (ed.), *Race, Class, and Gender in the United States: An Integrated Study*. New York: St. Martin's Press, 1992.

National Center for Education Statistics. *The Condition of Education, 1992*. Washington, D.C.: U.S. Department of Education, 1992.

National Committee on Pay Equity. "The Wage Gap: Myths and Facts." In P. S. Rothenburg (ed.), *Race, Class, and Gender in the United States: An Integrated Study*. New York: St. Martin's Press, 1992.

Omi, M., and Winant, H. "Racial Formations." In P. S. Rothenburg (ed.), *Race, Class, and Gender in the United States: An Integrated Study*. New York: St. Martin's Press, 1992.

Pearce, D. "Something Old, Something New: Women's Poverty in the 1990s." In S. Matteo (ed.), *American Women in the Nineties: Today's Critical Issues*. Boston: Northeastern University Press, 1993.

Rhode, D. "Gender Equity and Employment Policy." In S. Matteo (ed.), *American Women in the Nineties: Today's Critical Issues*. Boston: Northeastern University Press, 1993.

Ries, P., and Stone, A. J. (eds.). *The American Woman 1992–1993: A Status Report*. New York: W.W. Norton, 1992.

Rothenburg, P. S. (ed.). *Race, Class, and Gender in the United States: An Integrated Study*. New York: St. Martin's Press, 1992.

United States Bureau of the Census. *Statistical Abstract of the United States: 1992*. Washington, D.C.: U.S. Bureau of the Census, 1992.

United States Commission on Civil Rights. "The Problem: Discrimination." In P. S. Rothenburg (ed.), *Race, Class, and Gender in the United States: An Integrated Study*. New York: St. Martin's Press, 1992.

Wilkerson, I. "Black Life on Television: Realism or Stereotypes?" *The New York Times*, Aug. 15, 1993, Section 2, pp. 1, 28.

*ELISABETH HAYES is associate professor of continuing and vocational education at the University of Wisconsin–Madison.*

*SCIPIO A. J. COLIN III is assistant professor of adult and continuing education at North Carolina State University.*

*Knowledge building in adult education has resulted in biased and incomplete understandings of adults as learners.*

# Changing Dominant Understandings of Adults as Learners

*Daniele D. Flannery*

Our beliefs about adults as learners are reflected in our theories of adult learning and development, our everyday language, our decisions about content, our teaching methods, and the related research on teaching and learning that we do and promote. Implicitly and explicitly, adult education's prevailing beliefs about adult learners have supported racism and sexism. White male developmental models have been emphasized, and theories of learning that stress individualism, linear thinking, and Anglo European values of self-sufficiency have been generalized to all adults as "universal." This chapter examines the search for universal theories in adult education as a source of racism and sexism, suggests alternatives to universality that can provide adult education with new and more inclusive perspectives on adults as learners, and outlines the implications for adult education.

## Defining Racism and Sexism

Before beginning, it is important to clarify how the terms *racism* and *sexism* are used in this chapter. Racism is the thoughts, acts, and procedures of a system that bases the power of one group over another on skin color. In this chapter, the term refers to the power of white people over people of color. Sexism is the thoughts, acts, and procedures of a system that bases the power of one group over another on gender. In this chapter, the term refers to the power of males over females.

Racism and sexism are individual and collective behaviors that are manifest in our society. They are the result of historical processes and of individual and group socialization to various ways of thinking and behaving. They shape

NEW DIRECTIONS FOR ADULT AND CONTINUING EDUCATION, no. 61, Spring 1994  © Jossey-Bass Publishers

the ways in which people experience social relations and practices. Racism and sexism in the individual can be conscious and unconscious. Racism and sexism are "everyday" ways of thinking and behaving (Essed, 1991, p. 42). "'Everyday' racism and 'everyday' sexism are the integration of racism and sexism into everyday situations through practices (cognitive and behavioral) that activate underlying power relations" (Essed, 1991, p. 50).

The everyday racism and sexism on which this chapter focuses is the value placed on universality in knowledge building. Universality is promoted and valued when ways of understanding people, ideas, and events are seen as applicable to all. Two theoretical areas will be used to consider the everyday sexism and racism inherent in universality: adult development theory and aspects of adult learning theory.

## Universality

Universality is the search for a master narrative (Lyotard, 1984), a broad, objective depiction of universal truth. In this search, which is often referred to as the *scientific approach*, knowledge is conceived of as the objective apprehending of truth or fact. Knowledge building is the objective collection of related truths or facts about some particular phenomenon. The goal of knowledge building in the scientific approach is a whole, complete, and therefore dogmatic picture.

Two aspects of the seeking of universal truth in knowledge building are problematic: the errors of reasoning that result when we seek universal truth and the power that those who gather, determine, and disseminate these universal truths exercise.

**Errors of Reasoning.** Accepting the notion of universal truth as a norm for the construction of knowledge results in errors of reasoning that affect the application of knowledge in the teaching-learning exchange. Minnich (1990) suggests four types of errors: faulty generalization, circular reasoning, mystified concepts, and partial knowledge.

Universality involves faulty generalizations. It treats persons of a particular kind or group as the only ones who are significant, the only ones who can represent or set the standard for all humans (Minnich, 1990). Data are generalized to all. Collard and Stalker (1991) provide an example of faulty generalization: The classic work of London, Wenkert, and Hagstrom (1963) on participation and social class is often generalized to the total population, despite the fact that the sample was exclusively male.

In the process of circular reasoning, persons or theories end up where they started without recognizing what they have done. The standards of "good theory" are derived from particular theoretical works by a particular group, but they are then used as if they were generally, even universally, appropriate. For example, many North American adult learning theories distinguish between adults and children by assuming that adult learners are independent and self-directed. This assumption has become established as an element of "good adult learning theory." This assumption and others like it are cited as neutral grounds for the judging and evaluating of appropriate "good adult learning theory." This reasoning is circular. Adult learning theory that assumes adults are *not* self-directed is judged less good, instead of merely different.

Mystified concepts is the third error of universality. They result from the preceding errors. Mystified concepts are "ideas, notions, categories, and the like that are so deeply familiar they are rarely questioned" (Minnich, 1990, p. 51). Not only do their complex cultural meanings perpetuate the exclusion of what is different, but also we are socialized to think of these mystified concepts as the gauge against which we must measure ourselves. Often we are led to think and act against our own interests and commitments without realizing that we are doing it. For example, adult development theories based on Erikson's (1978) work on the stages of man stress identity formation as necessary before the development of intimacy. This idea implies a positive evaluation of persons who have a strong sense of established identity. The resulting concept can make many women appear inadequate. Research conducted primarily with white women demonstrates that some women develop a sense of intimacy before forming an identity and that for others intimacy and identity are integrally related (Gilligan, 1982; Baruch, Barnett, and Rivers, 1983).

The fourth error, partial knowledge, results from the fact that questions are asked and answered within a tradition in which thinking is persistently shaped and expressed by the other errors. Partial knowledge encompasses only a part of what is being studied. It does not seriously take into account what is encountered as different except by defining it in relation to what is known and valued. For example, in a chapter on fostering opportunities for self-direction, Brockett and Hiemstra (1991) acknowledge that in Japan the culture emphasizes the importance of the group, but then, without any evidence, they leap (p. 187) to the conclusion that "Japan appears to be in a transitional state where the sanctity of the group is being reevaluated in terms of individual needs and wishes."

**Power Relationships.** Those who gather, determine, and disseminate universal truths exercise an exclusive power. This power is hidden by the assumption that the knowledge builders and those whose lives are being studied are interacting. It also is concealed by the assumption that anyone can participate in knowledge building. This is not the case. There is not, and has not been, mutual influence. Rather, the knowledge builders use their own lenses to determine truth. Their ways of viewing life are influenced by their own culture, values, and expectations. Furthermore, standards for the building and dissemination of knowledge by such means as publication, teaching, and speaking restrict access to knowledge building to the like-minded. This means that truth is controlled by a few, an elite. For adult education in North America, knowledge building has been conducted primarily from the perspective and according to the standards of white, male, Western-European persons. Much of the resulting knowledge and current knowledge building is accordingly racist and sexist.

In summary, the presumption of universality results in errors of reasoning in which "only one group is being generalized from" and in power relationships where "one group speaks for, of, and to all of us" (Minnich, 1990, p. 53).

## Results of Seeking Universal Truth

As noted, the results of seeking universal truth are that a single group becomes significant, represents everyone, and sets the standard for behavior. In effect, proponents of universal truth value uniformity, ignore differences, and treat those who do not conform as inadequate. People and cultures are silenced, rendered invisible, treated as though they did not exist. These practices occur in everyday adult education, and their presence in adult learning theory can be demonstrated. In adult learning theory, the search for the universal has resulted in everyday racism and sexism because it has promoted the perspectives and power of a single group, whose members are white, middle-class, and often male, over the perspectives and power of others. Clearly, there is a need to move beyond the practices of racism and sexism in our everyday lives and in everyday adult education as well. There is a need to move "beyond silencing not only by listening to those who have been institutionally banished from the center to the margins, but by deconstructing [taking apart] those policies and practices that have historically encoded power, privilege, and marginality" (Weis and Fine, 1993, p. 1). In order to do this, we must first recognize the universality in theories of adult learning, and then we must engage in strategies to change the resulting biased and exclusive knowledge and practices.

## Universal Theories in Understanding Adults as Learners: Supporting Everyday Racism and Sexism

This section scrutinizes several works from adult development theory and adult learning theory for examples of everyday racism and sexism that have occurred in adult education as it has promoted universal theories of adults as learners. The works examined reflect the bias inherent in the emphasis that adult education has placed on the individual and individual autonomy.

**Motivational Theory.** Maslow's (1970) theory of human motivation and self-actualization is constantly used in workshops and texts. In Maslow's theory, human needs are arranged hierarchically. The highest level of this hierarchy deals with self-actualization, by which Maslow (1970) means the full use of a person's talents, capabilities, and potentialities. Maslow's (1970) studies were primarily of males. In his findings, male characteristics and values became the norm. This male bias is reflected, for example, in his description of the need for self-esteem as "a desire for strength, for achievement, for adequacy, for mastery and confidence, for competence in the face of the world, and for independence and freedom" (Maslow, 1970, p. 45). The need for self-esteem is clearly regarded as higher and more valuable than the need for affiliation, and the need for self-actualization is even higher than the need for self-esteem. At one point, Maslow acknowledged that self-actualization was not a characteristic of women. However, he encouraged women to reach their "feminine" fulfillments and then, if they could manage, to reach further for self-actualization. According to Maslow (1970, p. xvii), "It is possible for a woman to have all the specifically female fulfillments (being loved, having the home, having the baby) and *then,* without giving up any of the satisfactions already achieved, go on beyond femaleness to the full humanness that she shares with males, for example, the full development of her intelligence, of any talents she may have, and of her own particular idiosyncratic genius, of her own individual fulfillment."

In point of fact, women and men "have different organizing principles around which their psyches are structured" (Miller, 1986, p. 62). For women, the maintenance of the needs of love, affection, and belongingness is critically important. In fact, research has shown that many women place greater emphasis than men do on communion, that is, on the experience of living within a community of others. In contrast, men are more inclined than women toward agency, that is, concern with individual actions (Donelson and Gullahorn, 1977). Gilligan's work (1982) further suggests that empathy, intimacy, relationships, and an ethic of caring are integral to women's definition of self.

From these perspectives, Maslow's (1970) theory of motivation, which emphasizes self-actualization, in which the individual personality is separated from connectedness and relationship, has little relevance for the female world. It does not acknowledge and value female life experience (Tietze and Shakeshaft, 1982). To promote this theory as universal is everyday sexism.

**Adult Learning Theory.** In adult learning theory, andragogy and theories of self-directed learning have emphasized individual autonomy as a universal value. In andragogy, long espoused as the ideal for adult education, the purpose of adult education is to enhance the learner's personal growth as the learner determines. Fostering the adult's capabilities for self-direction is integral to the practice of andragogy. In the literature on self-directed learning, accepting responsibility for one's own learning is valued as a proactive approach to the learning process, and enhancing and developing the adult's capabilities for self-direction becomes the primary objective for teaching (Candy, 1991).

Essential to andragogy and self-directed learning is the assumption that all people should, can, or want to accept individual freedom in learning. Regardless of our setting, haven't we all said or thought, "I expected the learner to take responsibility for her learning," "I expected her to ask for help if it was needed," "I expected her to find a way of dealing with the conflict between child care and class attendance." Let's ask ourselves this: Whose ideas and beliefs are these? Are they universal? Do they really represent the values of all people? Do they really represent the way in which all adults learn?

In reality, learning theories based on individualism and autonomy reflect values and attributes that are primarily Western, white, middle-class, and male (Clark and Wilson, 1991). They "tend to be found in those cultures, such as ours, where high status is obtained by competitive individual achievement" (Keddie, 1980, p. 54). Individualism is not equally valued by all groups even within our own society. The value orientations and learning processes of persons of non-European cultural background, such as Mexican Americans, African Americans, Native Americans, and Canadian Indians, tend to be based on communal and collective values (Pratt, 1988). In contrast, Hmong adults show a need for explicit teacher direction paralleling the Hmong reliance on authority and leadership (Hvitfeld, 1986). Clearly, to continue to promote learning theories that have individual achievement as a universal goal is to continue everyday racism in adult education.

## Implications for Adult Education

The valuing of the universal in adult education must be changed. New perspectives must be developed to overcome the racism and sexism inherent in universal understandings of adults as learners. As adult educators, we must engage in an honest critique of our theories and our practices. First, the possibility of diverse "knowledges" must be raised. That is, there is not one "knowledge," not one single social reality, but many divergent "knowledges," each representing unique ways of understanding and experiencing reality. Among others, the knowledges of women (Hugo, 1990) and people of color (Ross-Gordon, Martin, and Briscoe, 1990; Cassara, 1990) have been missing from adult education's efforts to understand adults as learners. Second, the nature of desirable knowledge itself must be questioned. Universality is a discriminatory criterion because it extends and imposes theories on all people. It is time to move away from a unilateral construction of adult development and learning theory toward a multilayered and comparative construction of social realities. Third, if women and people of color were considered in the past, they tended to be considered only insofar as they were important for and related to white men. Women and people of color need to be considered on their own as human subjects. Fourth, in the past, adult education, tacitly assuming that there was only one culture, failed to attend to the relationships between a person's culture and a person's development and learning when considering adults as learners. This must change.

Practically, as adult educators we can do two things: We can think these issues through and become aware of the biases in the knowledge that we create and believe in, and we can plan to change our own approach to knowledge building.

## Strategies for Making Knowledge and Knowledge Building Sensitive to Diversity

As adult educators, we must become "engaged and transformative" intellectuals (Giroux and McLaren, 1989, p. xxiii). The following are offered as suggestions for beginning that process.

First, the notion that knowledge building is the right of a select group must be changed. We are all knowledge makers, not just those in academe. We have different experiences, and we have our own ways of making sense of life. That is knowledge building. We must claim our right to do this, and we must be prepared to see other individuals and groups do the same.

Second, the knowledge we and others build must be evaluated to protect against a narrow search for universal truth that in reality is biased and limited. I have found that a set of questions asked by Lather (1991, p. 84) is particularly helpful in critiquing the knowledge that I am building and the knowledge developed by others. For purposes of this article, I have combined those questions with my own.

Did I create a text that was multiple? That is, does my knowledge consider people of different gender, race, and experiences? Have I allowed differences to exist, accepting them as a valid part of reality rather than trying to place them in competition with each other? When I have not created a text that is multiple, have I clearly acknowledged that it is only about one group of people and that I do not know that it could be said of anyone else?

Have I thought through the knowledge in a way that makes sure that I haven't put my own way of thinking or believing forward as truth? Did I work at being open to see the importance of knowledge constructs different from my own? Have I included and cited such knowledge? Did I focus on the limits of my own conceptualizations? Did I include contrary experiences and ways of thinking? Have I had people with different experiences and values review my ideas for bias and limitations? How do I work through feelings of being threatened when opposing viewpoints challenge me? Regardless of how inclusive I feel that I am, do I ask people who are different from me how they perceive me? Do I have what it takes to hear what is said, or do I use reason to dismiss the feedback that I receive?

"Did my work multiply political spaces and prevent the concentration of power in any one point? Perhaps more importantly, did it go beyond critique to help in producing pluralized and diverse spaces for the emergence of subjugated knowledges and for the organization of resistance? . . . What has been muted, repressed, unheard? How has what I've done shaped, subverted, complicated? Have I confronted my own evasions and raised doubts about any illusions of closure?" (Lather, 1991, p. 84).

Does the theory promote similarities within differences? Does it value the differences while seeking common elements in peoples' struggle against oppression and exclusion?

Third, remember that knowledge is both created and transmitted in the teaching-learning exchange. Questions not unlike the ones just voiced must be asked about the knowledge that we promote in our teaching. Do we assume universals in what we teach without checking them out? To help ourselves, we can ask a three-part question: What does adult education believe about X? Does it imply or state that the belief applies to all people? And is it true that the belief applies to all people? Begin to answer the third question by openly reflecting on your own practice. For example, are the people in your teaching-learning experiences really motivated by self-actualization? Answer the question by reading and asking people. What is written and said about women and people of color with regard to the belief that you are questioning?

Look at your own personal behaviors in and out of the teaching-learning exchange. Do they demonstrate that you accept universal theories about adults as learners? For example, recently, I overheard one adult basic education (ABE) teacher say to another, "Oh, don't pay attention to the Hispanics in the class. They don't want to learn. They just come here to be together and socialize." The ABE teacher held a universal belief that learners who want to learn listen to the instructor and do not interact. The ABE teacher dismissed the possibility that there are other ways of learning and that the Hispanics in the class might be demonstrating their learning style—a collaborative style in which learning is accomplished by sharing and in particular by sharing personal meaningful experiences.

Fourth, work to change and broaden your own knowledge base. Attend to persons and knowledges that theories about adults as learners have excluded.

Search text sources for accounts of diverse kinds of people and experiences. For example, use Gordon Parks's *The Learning Tree* (1963) or Maxine Hong Kingston's *The Woman Warrior* (1987) to broaden traditional North American perspectives on human maturation.

In your classes and curricula, listen to the missing voices. Pay attention to all people and groups. Allow them to tell the diverse stories of how and where they learn and what they value in learning.

Search out people with diverse backgrounds. Talk with teachers and learners of different races or the other gender. Work to listen and understand the "basic assumptions, perceptions, motivation, nonverbal language, feelings, defenses, basic needs, conflicts, cultural norms, and patterns of behavior common to the cultures" (Briscoe and Ross, 1989, p. 587) of women and people of color. Learn what is important knowledge for them and how they make knowledge.

## Conclusion

If we as adult educators choose to promote successful learning for all people, it is clear that we must purge all elements of everyday sexism and racism from our beliefs about and practices toward adults as learners. To do so, we must change the valuing of the universal that has prevailed in the literature on knowledge building in adult learning. Instead, we must acquire new perspectives on adults as learners that include women and people of color. The author hopes that this chapter will be the beginning of further reflection, discussion, and challenge on this topic.

## References

Baruch, G. K., Barnett, R. C., and Rivers, C. *Lifeprints*. New York: McGraw-Hill, 1983.

Briscoe, D. B., and Ross, J. M. "Racial and Ethnic Minorities and Adult Education." In S. B. Merriam and P. M. Cunningham (eds.), *Handbook of Adult and Continuing Education*. San Francisco: Jossey-Bass, 1989.

Brockett, R. G. and Hiemstra, R. *Self-Direction in Adult Learning*. London: Routledge, 1991.

Candy, P. C. *Self-Direction for Lifelong Learning: A Comprehensive Guide to Theory and Practice*. San Francisco: Jossey-Bass, 1991.

Cassara, B. B. (ed.). *Adult Education in a Multicultural Society*. New York: Routledge, 1990.

Clark, M. C., and Wilson, A. L. "Context and Rationality in Mezirow's Theory of Transformational Learning." *Adult Education Quarterly*, 1991, 41 (2), 75–91.

Collard, S., and Stalker, J. "Women's Trouble: Women, Gender, and the Learning Environment." In R. Hiemstra (ed.), *Creating Environments for Effective Adult Learning*. New Directions for Adult and Continuing Education, no. 50. San Francisco: Jossey-Bass, 1991.

Donelson, E., and Gullahorn, J. E. *Women: A Psychological Perspective*. New York: Wiley, 1977.

Erikson, E. H. *Adulthood*. New York: W.W. Norton, 1978.

Essed, P. *Understanding Everyday Racism: An Interdisciplinary Theory*. Newbury Park, Calif.: Sage, 1991.

Gilligan, C. *In a Different Voice: Psychological Theory and Women's Development*. Cambridge, Mass.: Harvard University Press, 1982.

Giroux, H. A., and McLaren, P. (eds.). *Critical Pedagogy, the State, and Cultural Struggle*. New York: State University of New York, 1989.

Hugo, J. M. "Adult Education History and the Issue of Gender: Toward a Different History of Adult Education in America." *Adult Education Quarterly*, 1990, 41, 1–16.

Hvitfeld, C. "Traditional Culture, Perceptual Style, and Learning: The Classroom Behavior of Hmong Adults." *Adult Education Quarterly*, 1986, 36 (2), 65–77.

Keddie, N. "Adult Education: An Ideology of Individualism." In J. L. Thompson (ed.), *Adult Education for Change*. London: Hutchinson, 1980.

Kingston, M. H. *The Woman Warrior*. Bloomington: Indiana University Press, 1987.

Lather, P. *Getting Smart: Feminist Research and Pedagogy with/in the Postmodern*. New York: Routledge, 1991.

London, J., Wenkert, R., and Hagstrom, W. *Adult Education and Social Class*. Berkeley: Survey Research Center, University of California, 1963.

Lyotard, J. *The Postmodern Condition: A Report on Knowledge*. (G. Bennington and B. Massumi, trans.) Minneapolis: University of Minnesota Press, 1984.

Maslow, A. H. *Motivation and Personality*. (2nd ed.) New York: HarperCollins, 1970.

Miller, J. B. *Toward a New Psychology of Women*. (2nd ed.) Boston: Beacon Press, 1986.

Minnich, E. K. *Transforming Knowledge*. Philadelphia: Temple University Press, 1990.

Parks, G. *The Learning Tree*. New York: HarperCollins, 1963.

Pratt, D. "Cross-Cultural Relevance of Selected Psychological Perspectives on Learning." In M. Zukas (ed.), *Proceedings of Transatlantic Dialogue: A Research Exchange*. Leeds, England: University of Leeds, 1988.

Ross-Gordon, J. M., Martin, L. G., and Briscoe, D. B. (eds.). *Serving Culturally Diverse Populations.* New Directions for Adult and Continuing Education, no. 48. San Francisco: Jossey-Bass, 1990.

Tietze, I. N., and Shakeshaft, C. "Toward a Reconstruction of Organizational Theory: Androcentric Bias in A. H. Maslow's Theory of Human Motivation and Self-Actualization." Paper presented at the annual meeting of the American Educational Research Association, New York, 1982.

Weis, L. and Fine, M. (eds.). *Beyond Silenced Voices: Class, Race, and Gender in United States Schools.* Albany: State University of New York, 1993.

*DANIELE D. FLANNERY is assistant professor of adult education and coordinator of the adult education Doctor of Education program at The Pennsylvania State University, Harrisburg.*

*Marginalization occurs when one person's views are valued and voiced at the sociopolitical and historical expense of others. Understanding the individual's polyrhythmic reality gives us a way of giving voice to the multiple and varied realities found in the classroom.*

# Giving Voice: An Inclusive Model of Instruction—A Womanist Perspective

*Vanessa Sheared*

> Be the best! If you are a thief, be the best one that you can be. If you are a doctor, be the best.
> —Ms. Jones, seventh-grade teacher

These words are ingrained in my memory. To the ordinary reader, they might not mean very much, but to that seventh grader who heard these words, the meaning was quite clear. For me growing up in one of the many varied communities on the south side of Chicago, these words reflected the reality of the many faces and voices in that classroom. This teacher knew that some children would go on to become teachers, lawyers, doctors, and entrepreneurs. And she knew that others would live their lives in constant retreat from the law. She understood their differing worlds and realities, and she interpreted and reflected these realities in the words that she spoke.

As adult educators, we do not always get an opportunity to encourage our students to become the best that they can be. Their worlds, ideas, perceptions, and values have already been molded, perhaps by someone like the teacher whom I encountered at the impressionable age of twelve. So what is the role of the adult educator? Is it to continue to mold the worlds of students? Or are we to become instruments through which our students begin to reflect on the multiple and varied realities that they, like we, bring to the classroom? And if the latter is the case, then through what means must we instruct them?

Educators in general and adult educators in particular are becoming increasingly concerned by the question, How are we to deliver course content in such a way that classroom discourse acknowledges all voices—the multiple ways in which people interpret and reflect their understandings of the world? Multiculturalism, Africentrism,[1] bilingualism, feminism, womanism, perspective transformation, critical consciousness, cooperative learning are just some of the methods and theoretical constructs that adult educators have explored or are currently exploring and implementing (Colin and Preciphs, 1991; Freire, 1970; Hayes, 1989; Mezirow, 1978; Ross-Gordon, 1991). Each of these methods and constructs reflects an attempt to give voice to political, economic, and social life stories, experiences, cultures, and histories that have been excluded from the educational mainstream.

This chapter has three goals: to introduce the womanist critique into the discourse on gender and race in adult education, to challenge adult educators to incorporate polyrhythmic realities into their instructional practices, and to define the role and purpose of education by offering a womanist instructional methodology intended to give voice to those whom traditional and unidimensional methods of instruction have silenced.

The womanist methodology acknowledges the ways in which the polyrhythmic realities (Barkley-Brown, 1988) of the instructor and students help to shape the learning environment. These polyrhythmic realities either limit or increase the individual's ability to engage in critical reflective learning at a given moment in time. The concept of polyrhythmic reality reflects the belief that individuals do not just have multiple realities and distinct understandings of them. Instead, individuals experience intersecting realities simultaneously—their realities are polyrhythmic. This concept represents a radical departure from Western, linear notions of the world and reality. Polyrhythms are characteristic of the aesthetic sense as reflected in African American art, music, and dance, as well as language. Barkley-Brown (1988, pp. 11–12) describes this aesthetic in African American quilts as "creating the impression of several patterns moving in different directions or multiple rhythms within the context of a controlled design. . . . The symmetry in African-American quilts does not come from uniformity as it does in Euro-American quilts; rather, the symmetry comes through the diversity." Applying the concept to individuals, she suggests the importance of recognizing that "people and actions do move in multiple directions at once. If we analyze these people and actions by linear models, we will create dichotomies, ambiguities, cognitive dissonance, disorientation, and confusion in places where none exist" (Barkley-Brown, 1988, pp. 17–18).

This concept is analogous to the womanist perspective proposed by Walker (1984). The womanist perspective seeks to expose the differences and similarities that human beings experience in the classroom as a result of skin color, language, economic status, and personal experiences. These experiences are relevant to individuals' social, cultural, political, and historical understanding of themselves in relation to others. According to Williams (1990, p. 70), use of the term *womanist* represents a "commitment to the survival and wholeness of entire people—men and women." I believe that the womanist perspective is more inclusive and that it challenges us to think critically about such issues as racism, sexism, language, religious orientation, and sexual orientation. More important, its aim is to reinterpret the word—the ways in which we read, hear, and ultimately speak and listen to one another. This perspective, along with its corresponding relationship to giving voice, will be discussed more fully in this chapter. The discussion that follows is intended to be relevant for all practitioners in adult education programs, whether they work in adult literacy classes, adult graduate programs, or training programs. The terms *Africentric feminist* and *womanist* are used interchangeably throughout this discussion.

## Silencing of Others

Since the 1960s, historians, educators, political activists, and others have raised concerns that the contributions of women, African Americans, and other groups to the historical, economical, and political development of the United States are invisible. Studies on gender and race have shown that the exclusion of these groups from written texts has silenced their voices. While the primary focus has been on the silencing by the dominant culture of others' voices in written texts, concerns also have been raised about the silencing of voices in public speaking.

The Africentric feminist perspective is not just about the voices that have been silenced on the grounds of race or gender but instead considers the simultaneous effects of race and gender (Collins, 1990). While both Africentric and feminist scholars discuss the silencing of voices and marginalization, Africentric feminist scholars suggest that Africentric scholars and feminist scholars fail to address both gender and race as a unifying whole (Collins, 1991; hooks, 1984). As a result, the black woman's voice, as well as other marginalized voices, has been silenced. Wallace (1990, p. 70) asserts that "there is no question . . . that the unrelenting logic of dualism or polar opposition, such as black and white, good and evil, male and female, is basic to the discourse of the dominant culture and tends to automatically erase black female subjectivity." Thus, black women's issues become secondary to the dominant discourse on race, gender, and class.

## The Womanist Perspective

The womanist perspective acknowledges the intertwining realities that human beings experience within society. Race, gender, and class are interwoven. The relationship between race, gender, class, and the womanist perspective can best be illustrated with a triangle. Race, gender, and class are intersecting lines of reality, and the womanist perspective views these realities from within the triangle. The womanist perspective is grounded in the African American woman's marginalized status in relation to race, gender, and class.

Although her experiences are grounded in this experience, her reality is shaped by others. The womanist perspective is born of a direct response to the exclusion of the African American woman's voice from the discourse on race, gender, and class. Many European American feminist scholars as well as scholars engaged in the discourse on race would say that, when they speak on issues related to women or race, they include the voice of the African American woman. However, African American feminist scholars do not believe this to be true (Collins, 1990; Dill, 1990; King, 1990).

Some African American women scholars use the term *feminist*, while others use the term *womanist*. Many have used the term *womanist* to reflect an understanding of race, gender, and class that is grounded in "a commitment to the survival and wholeness of entire people—men and women—as well as "to a valorization of women's works in all their varieties and multitudes" (Williams, 1990, p. 70). People's race, gender, ethnicity, sexual preference, and religious orientation must be acknowledged and examined for individuals to be recognized in their fullness as interconnected human beings.

"Black women," as opposed to "blacks and women," is used by Africentric feminist scholars to indicate that African American women are not "both/or" but rather "both/and." King (cited by Collins, 1990, p. 309) has described the both/and orientation as "the act of being simultaneously a member of a group and yet standing apart from it." The experience of African American women has been further described as the other of the other (Wallace, 1990). According to this perspective, African American women's voices have been silenced because the discourse on race and gender has negated their significance. It excludes their unique experiences in favor of the larger good (Sheared, 1992).

A both/and nondichotomous relationship represents the wholeness and the connectedness of entire people. It does not tear them apart. It is grounded in an understanding of what King (1990) describes as a double or multiple consciousness that develops as a result of the multiple jeopardies that women and blacks have experienced historically, socially, and economically. The womanist perspective shapes the both/and reality into a connected polyrhythmic whole. We no longer see ourselves as separate beings but as communal spirits. We are more than black and woman. We are black women connected to all brothers and sisters engaged in the struggle against oppression based on race, gender, and class.

## A Womanist Perspective on Adult Education

Many marginalized or underrepresented adult students enrolled in adult education classes confront the experience that King (1990) describes as both/or and Wallace (1990) as the other of the other—that is, the individual's voice is negated as the result of being grouped with others on the basis of similarities in race and gender. Each student brings a set of experiences to the learning environment that reflects his or her status at work and at home and within his or her family, his or her relative positions in time (history), and his or her understandings of these factors. Polyrhythmic reality reflects the wholeness, the uniqueness, and—most important—the connectedness of individuals to others in society, their both/and realities.

Barkley-Brown (1990) has described quilting by African American women as analogous to what occurs between teachers and students in the classroom. It is useful in helping us to understand the relationship of instruction to both/and reality. First, the designs used in these quilts are not necessarily symmetrically organized. Instead, the quilting reflects an aesthetic understanding by the makers of what the quilt represents for them in their everyday experience. For instance, pieces of cloth from old family clothes and heirlooms are used to represent an interconnectedness that goes beyond the confines of geometrically correct forms. The shape of the quilt results from the meanings that individual quilters give to the pieces that compose it. Barkley-Brown (1990) uses the Creole term *gumbo ya ya*—everybody talking at once—to describe this art form.

African American women's quilting and gumbo ya ya can be used to describe what Barkley-Brown (1990) calls the polyrhythmic way of understanding. In other words, rather than espousing one uniform center or reality, the student and the teacher embrace multiple or dualistic realities. The teacher must decenter or disempower himself or herself in order to empower the students. The teacher allows students to seek and interpret their world and their words in a political, social, historical, and economic context. The self is understood in relation to its connectedness with others and their perceptions of reality. The process is a communal experience.

Our goal as adult educators is to find ways in which we can uncover and acknowledge the voice of each student; to recognize that we, like our students, bring polyrhythmic realities to the learning environment; to find ways of disempowering ourselves in the learning environment so that students begin to take responsibility for their learning; and to understand that the information we proffer is grounded in a political, social, historical, sexual, racial, and economical context that is unique to us (in other words, we recognize that our subjective understandings of the world are different yet interconnected).

How is this learning environment created? The next section describes a process that adult educators can use to create a learning environment that meets the goals just outlined.

## Giving Voice

As noted earlier, giving voice has become an aim of those who seek to provide students and educators with an opportunity to become engaged in a critically reflective dialogue regardless of the subject matter. This aim is based on the proposition that all knowledge is grounded in a social, political, economic, and historical context. To give voice requires us to acknowledge different realities and understand that there are different ways of interpreting reality. "Voice is related to the means whereby teachers and students attempt to make themselves present in history and to define themselves as active authors of their own worlds" (Weiler, 1989, p. xiii). According to this author, it "represents those multiple subjectivities, discourses, and biographies that constitute teachers and students alike within relations of power, history, and experience" (Weiler, 1989, p. xiii). Giroux and McLaren (1986, p. 235) state that the "concept of voice constitutes the focal point for a theory of teaching and learning . . . as well as new and challenging ways of confronting and engaging in everyday life." Voice is the active engagement of students and teachers in dialogue with one another. Both are heard and "define themselves as active authors of their worlds . . . it is the unique instance of self-expression through which students affirm their own class, cultural, racial, and gender identities" (Giroux and McLaren, 1986, p. 235).

Quite simply, giving voice allows students and teachers to engage and disengage in polyrhythmic realities. Giroux and McLaren (1986, p. 235) concluded that voice is not static but rather used "to make ourselves understood and listened to and to define ourselves as active participants in the world." An Africentric feminist analysis acknowledges voice in the contextual framework of social class, historical and political hegemony, and its relationship with gender and racial oppression. It recognizes but does not negate the realities of both the oppressed and the oppressor, the learned and the learner.

My research (Sheared, 1992) incorporates the Africentric feminist epistemology (Collins, 1990, 1991) because it clearly communicates the oppositional worldview that was essential to understanding the educational, political, and social realities of African American women receiving public assistance. The Africentric feminist epistemology diminishes the negative effects of what King (1990) describes as multiple consciousness and the both/or orientation. It supports Dill's (1990) dialectics of black womanhood and Wallace's (1990) other of the other. The Africentric episteme allows the stories of African American women to be told in ways that do not tear apart or objectify their lives. It also does not obfuscate or mystify the words that they use to interpret and understand the word and the world.

Collins (1990, 1991) depicts the Africentric epistemology as a method that Africentric scholars can use to uncover and describe knowledge produced within the African diaspora. I believe that adult educators can use the following process to reach the goal of giving voice to the many realities that students bring to the learning environment. The process is grounded in two epistemological and two axiological assumptions.

*Concrete experience is used as a criterion of meaning.* This assumption acknowledges that there is more than one way of knowing. Both knowledge and wisdom are important. Knowledge is grounded in the individual's race, gender, and class. Knowledge consists of one's everyday lived experiences and understandings of that reality in terms of dominance and authority. In contrast, wisdom is what one uses to read, interpret, and speak in order to survive, given the information that one receives.

Collins (1990) concludes that the narrative method is one way of uncovering the criterion of meaning. An individual's words tell her or his story and are narrated either in print or by voice. The story is "not torn apart in analysis, and trusted as core belief, not admired as science" (Collins, 1990, p. 312). Students are given an opportunity to read and listen to the words that they use to describe a particular event or a skill that they use to accomplish a particular task. Ultimately, the way in which students read and interpret the symbols used to communicate information must change. They must act on that information in the class, on the job, or in their personal life.

For example, math learning for literacy students can be enhanced if students talk about the mathematical skills that they use in their everyday lives. These skills can include measuring ingredients for cooking and determining the distance between point A and point B or the time that it takes to prepare and cook a certain dish. These skills can be incorporated into a lesson on counting, addition, or subtraction skills. Discussion of these concepts in relationship to everyday examples enables the teacher and others in the class to introduce ways in which numbers and simple mathematical processes affect us in a political, social, economical, and historical context. For example, questions can be asked about the ways in which escalating costs have affected people's ability to prepare certain meals. How do they affect the learner and his or her ability to purchase ingredients? What can the learner do or what has the learner done to change his or her ability to purchase the products needed? This is just one example of the way in which individuals' concrete frame of reference can be used either to teach new skills or to show learners that they already have the power or information necessary to create change within their own environment.

*Dialogue is the basis for assessing knowledge claims.* A primary epistemological assumption is that connectedness rather than separation is essential to the knowledge validation process. Collins (1990, p. 317) concludes that the use of dialogue for African American women might be a way of "invoking a particular female way of knowing." Belenky, Clinchy, Goldberger, and Tarule (1986) list several ways in which women construct their realities about truth, knowledge, and authority. They conclude that women proceed through several stages as they move from silence to an ability to construct knowledge. They contend that these stages illustrate that women move from a position of total subordination to one in which they share equal voice, or connectedness, in the decisions and choices that they make. Dialoguing gives students an opportunity to challenge the knowledge constructed by others. In so doing, they apply their own understanding to determine what needs to be done.

As students dialogue with one another, they begin to explore alternative ways of viewing the world. More important, they begin to voice their under-standing of the ways in which they have learned to operate within the world. If we return to the example just used, math students begin to see how the mathematical skills that they have used affect their lives while at the same time learning new ways of using skills to create changes in their lives.

*An ethic of caring emphasizes the uniqueness of individuals, elicits appropriate emotion from the dialogue, and recognizes empathetic understanding.* The three ele-ments of an ethic of caring permeate African American culture. One example is the call-and-response discourse that many African American preachers have used in churches. The minister is responsible for pointing out principles from the Bible in a way that evokes a response of understanding from the congre-gation. Both the affective and the cognitive domains are involved. The process goes beyond simple questions and answers to questions that invoke complex responses. Moreover, the preacher shares a part of himself with the congrega-tion. He must be willing to listen to its responses, react, and then follow up with responses that suggest he understands them as well as they understand him. In other words, the minister and the congregation talk back and forth to each other. It represents an interconnectedness based on an understanding of the meanings that they each have of what they hear and observe in that moment.

For educators, an ethic of caring creates an environment in which partic-ipants come to an interconnected state of being through call and response. The question and the answer determine the level of trust and caring that is neces-sary if learning is to occur.

*An ethic of personal accountability guides both teaching and learning.* Not only must individuals develop their knowledge claims through dialogue, but they must present these claims in a style proving their concern for their ideas. Peo-ple are held accountable for their claims of knowledge. Learners must be held accountable for what they want to learn. The teacher is accountable for struc-turing the learning experience and enabling the students. In other words, the responsibility for learning is not just the domain of the teacher but of the learner as well.

I used this method in a course titled "Educating Disadvantaged Adults." In one activity, students were asked to rethink the title of the course in rela-tionship to the materials that they read (the narration) and the discourse that had occurred in class (the dialogue). Each student was responsible for rethink-ing and renaming the course. Students worked individually and in groups to uncover their own biases and the impact that these had on the ways they thought and taught those whom they considered to be disadvantaged. At the end of the course, each student presented his or her title to the entire group. Students were given an opportunity to question and respond to the ideas pre-sented.

At the end of the course, students acknowledged that they had changed their opinions about who the disadvantaged were. They also stated that they had begun to change the way in which they taught them—because they no longer saw them as beings outside and unconnected to who they were. No longer did my students dichotomize *us* and *them*. It became *we* as the term *disadvantaged* became relative. It helped them to gain an understanding of their political, economical, social, and historical being and its connectedness to their race, gender, and class status. Change had occurred not only in students' thought but in their proposed behavior.

## Conclusion

Although the womanist method helps us to understand and grapple with our polyrhythmic realities, it is in no way meant to be the only method that educators use to help their students activate their voices in the confines of formal and informal educational settings. To limit ourselves to one methodological paradigm risks silencing those to whom we hope to give voice. As long as we couch issues in the terms of a black cause or white woman's cause, we maintain the risk of negating black women as well as others. In other words, the womanist perspective must be placed in a context that allows voices to be heard and specific content information to be learned. Alternative instructional methods need to note this caveat: "Feminist readings can lead to misapprehensions of particular or even of a whole tradition, but certain of its formulations offer us a vocabulary that can be meaningful in terms of our own experience. Feminist theory . . . offers us not only the possibility of changing one's reading of the world but of changing the world itself" (Wallace, 1990, p. 68).

The womanist perspective is aimed at aiding the instructional process, not at becoming the content. Giving voice acknowledges that there are multiple ways of presenting and interpreting information and knowledge. This then means that one accepts and celebrates the polyrhythmic realities of both the student and the teacher in the learning environment.

As a final recommendation, before any adult educator initiates a particular method or model, she or he should engage in the following call and response activity. I have provided  some suggested responses, but your own may vary.

CALL: What is my role and goal as an adult educator?
RESPONSE: I believe that my role and my goal as an adult educator is to help students reflect on the multiple realities of gender, race, and class and their relationship to history, socioeconomics, and politics. More important, I should seek not only to uncover discrepancies and injustices within our educational process, but I must seek to help create environments for change.
CALL: Should my role be primarily to shape and mold the worlds of students, or should I become an instrument through which students begin to reflect on the polyrhythmic realities that they and I bring to the classroom environment?

RESPONSE: I am not here to shape or mold my students' thinking, but I am here to be used as a vessel to help students uncover the polyrhythmic realities that they and I possess in the learning environment.

CALL: Through what means must I instruct them?

RESPONSE: I must learn to give voice to my students. Giving voice occurs as a result of me decentering and centering self along with my students. Together we develop new meanings, understandings, and ways of thinking about the world and the word. In other words " we must pivot" the center in order to center in another's experience (Aptheker, 1989, Barkley-Brown, 1990). The dignity and rights of all—men and women—must be valued through the way we teach, speak, and interact with one another.

If your responses are similar to the ones shown here, then you should review readings and materials aimed at giving voice to your students. Some of the references used in this chapter can help you to begin this process.

## Note

1. The use of *Africentrism* rather than the more common *Afrocentrism* is explained in the Editors' Notes.

## References

Aptheker, B. *Tapestries of Life*. Amherst: University of Massachusetts Press, 1989.

Barkley-Brown, E. "African American Women's Quilting: A Framework for Conceptualizing and Teaching African American Women's History." In M. Malson, E. Mudimbe-Boyi, J. O'Barr, and M. Wyer (eds.), *Black Women in America: Social Science Perspectives*. Chicago: University of Chicago Press, 1990.

Belenky, M., Clinchy, B., Goldberger, N. R., and Tarule, J. M. *Women's Ways of Knowing: The Development of Self, Voice, and Mind*. New York: Basic Books, 1986.

Colin, S.A.J., III, and Preciphs, T. K. "Perceptual Patterns and the Learning Environment: Confronting White Racism." In R. Hiemstra (ed.), *Creating Environments for Effective Adult Learning*. New Directions for Adult and Continuing Education, no. 50. San Francisco: Jossey-Bass, 1991.

Collins, P. H. "The Social Construction of Black Feminist Thought." In M. Malson, E. Mudimbe-Boyi, J. O'Barr, and M. Wyer (eds.), *Black Women in America: Social Science Perspectives*. Chicago: University of Chicago Press, 1990.

Collins, P. H. *Black Feminist Thought*. New York: Routledge, 1991.

Dill, B. T. "The Dialectics of Black Womanhood." In M. Malson, E., Mudimbe-Boyi, J. O'Barr, and M. Wyer (eds.), *Black Women in America: Social Science Perspectives*. Chicago: University of Chicago Press, 1990.

Freire, P. *Pedagogy of the Oppressed*. New York: Herder and Herder, 1970.

Giroux, H. A., and McLaren, P. "Teacher Education and the Politics of Engagement: The Case for Democratic Schooling." *Harvard Educational Review*, 1986, 56 (3), 213–238.

Hayes, E. "Insights from Women's Experiences for Teaching and Learning." In E. Hayes (ed.), *Effective Teaching Styles*. New Directions for Continuing Education, no. 43. San Francisco: Jossey-Bass, 1989.

hooks, b. *From Margin to Center*. Boston: South End Press, 1984.

King, D. K. "Multiple Jeopardy, Multiple Consciousness: The Context of Black Feminist Ideology." In M. Malson, E. Mudimbe-Boyi, J. O'Barr, and M. Wyer (eds.), *Black Women in America: Social Science Perspectives.* Chicago: University of Chicago Press, 1990.

Mezirow, J. "Perspective Transformation." *Adult Education,* 1978, *18* (2), 100–110.

Ross-Gordon, J. M. "Needed: A Multicultural Perspective for Adult Education Research." *Adult Education Quarterly,* 1991, *42* (1), 1–16.

Sheared, V. "From Workfare to Edfare: African American Women and the Elusive Quest for Self-Determination." Unpublished doctoral dissertation, Department of Leadership and Educational Policy Studies, Northern Illinois University, 1992.

Wallace, M. "Variations on Negation and the Heresy of Black Feminist Creativity." In H. Gates (ed.), *Reading Black, Reading Feminist: A Critical Anthology.* New York: Meridian Books, 1990.

Walker, A. *In Search of Our Mother's Gardens.* San Diego, Calif. Harcourt Brace Jovanovich, 1984.

Weiler, K. *Women Teaching for Change (Gender, Class, and Power).* Boston: Bergin and Garvey, 1989.

Williams, S. A. "Some Implications of Womanist Theory." In H. Gates (ed.), *Reading Black, Reading Feminist: A Critical Anthology.* New York: Meridian Books, 1990.

*VANESSA SHEARED is assistant professor of adult continuing education in the Center for Adult Education at San Francisco State University.*

*How can staff development be used to address issues of race and gender in adult education settings?*

# Staff Development: Addressing Issues of Race and Gender

*Donna D. Amstutz*

Staff development can address issues of racism and sexism in adult education. One goal of staff development can be to encourage culturally responsive education and training by giving attention to the cultural experiences of adult educators, their students, and coworkers. This chapter begins by addressing racist and sexist aspects of instruction and interaction with adult learners. The general need for staff development to overcome racism and sexism is illustrated with examples from current practice. Regardless of the emphasis of specific programs—literacy volunteer training, military education, leadership development, human resource development, continuing professional education—educational activities and staff should demonstrate a sensitivity to issues of race and gender. Specific formal and informal strategies that can be used to address racist and sexist behaviors are discussed. The chapter concludes with some cautions and challenges for adult educators.

## The Nature of Staff Development

Historically, staff development was intended primarily to address deficiencies in teachers' knowledge and skills. Staff development programs were designed to define deficiencies in teacher knowledge and skills, identify deficient teachers, and remedy their deficiencies through mandatory attendance at workshops. This approach has often resulted in formal workshops that may or may not have the intended effect. It is used most appropriately when specific information is to be presented. Some adult education programs, particularly in adult basic education, correctional education, and continuing professional education, continue to operate from this philosophy.

A view of staff development that challenged the deficit scenario emerged in the early 1970s. Jackson (1971) called for recognizing teachers from a humanistic, not mechanistic, perspective. Labeled the *growth approach*, this view held staff development to be "an imaginative, inventive ongoing process, not a singular event" (Orlich, 1989, p. 8). Since this perspective views staff development as a process, not a program, it should account both for the individual needs of adult educators and for the policy needs of the institutions in which they work.

This chapter assumes that staff development should be based on the growth approach. The words *staff development* are purposefully used to include education for all staff members of an adult education program, whether they are classified as professionals or not. Any staff interacting with adult learners can have a significant effect on the tone of the cultural context in which learning takes place.

Staff development should enable educators to think critically about cultural dynamics. *Culture* has been defined as the beliefs, customs, and other products of human work and thought created by a people or group (American Heritage Dictionary, 1983). One individual is never a complete representation of a culture. One Asian American adult learner does not represent all Asian American adult learners. The interaction of many dynamics determines cultural identity. Race, ethnicity, gender, and class are not independent or isolated characteristics of an individual. According to Gollnick (1992), every person is a complex mix of many cultural factors. Acknowledging and valuing individuals, not merely the specific racial group or gender to which they belong, is another objective of staff development that attempts to address these issues.

## Racism and Sexism in Adult Education

While many adult educators pride themselves on being nonsexist and nonracist, examination of actual behaviors reveals the extent to which individual actions could be interpreted as sexist or racist. The examples that follow were taken from the author's experiences and therefore relate primarily to the adult education professorate. However, the racist or sexist behaviors and interpretations could easily have occurred in other adult education settings.

At a Commission of Professors of Adult Education meeting, two assistant professors proposed a preconference on African American research issues. A member of the executive committee responded immediately, "Oh, but it must have high quality and be research based." One interpretation is that the executive committee member could have made that comment in relation to any suggested topic. Since the actual statement makes no reference to racist beliefs, some people would not have known that the statement could be racist. Another interpretation, by people who have had different experiences, is that the executive committee member assumed that the preconference would not have high quality and that it would not be research based because it related to a minority group. From this perspective, the statement indicated that the executive committee member in question, who certainly did not view herself as racist, was operating under racist assumptions. While the executive committee member may not have intended to offend the two assistant professors, their interpretation was based on the actual statement, not on knowledge of her intention. Issues of race and gender are situated in the discrepancy between the two interpretations. Sensitivity to the gaps between intention and interpretation is an area for growth in understanding the cultural context of interactions.

An adult basic education (ABE) instructor became concerned that most women in the community college program where she worked were referred to clerical or other entry-level office training programs. She began to ask why the women, who were primarily single mothers, were not referred to higher-paying training programs, such as carpentry apprenticeships, real estate sales, or diesel repair. When she questioned the other instructors (primarily female) at a staff development activity, they admitted that they had assumed that the women wanted to be secretaries or clerks and never suggested alternatives that have better earning potential. Gender discrimination is not always perpetuated by males. Errors of omission (in this case errors involving alternative vocational programs) can result in unintentional discrimination. When the instructors recognized their unstated biases and the resulting omissions, they were able to begin to monitor their own practices in order to achieve gender equity.

While teaching in a program that served a primarily African American graduate student population in Chicago, an adult education professor presented the mainstream justification for family literacy programs. The rationale cited in the literature is that students who come from highly literate families tend to produce highly educated children. Only after the African American graduate students questioned this rationale did the professor indicate that the studies on which the rationale was based were conducted on primarily white, middle-class families. In the light of their experiences, the graduate students believed that the determining factor was the value that the parents attached to literacy, not the presence of a literate parent. Since most of the minority graduate students had parents or grandparents who were illiterate as a result of historical discrimination, their reality differed from the people who had been the subjects of study. If the professor had not been open to viewpoints from other cultures, a competing theory for family literacy would have been overlooked. Moreover, the minority group did not see their experience validated through research or discussion.

In a similar instance, a white male professor discussed several theories of adult development that are rather standard in graduate classes. He prefaced his discussion by saying that the studies were based on white, middle-class, usually successful males, but he presented the traditional theories nonetheless. For many minorities and females in his class, the disclaimer helped them to assess the usefulness of the theories presented. However, the disclaimer did nothing to identify development theories that may more accurately reflect the students' experiences. The professor did not take the necessary step of identifying relevant writings on the development of women and minorities. Omission of some information can be interpreted as confirming the superiority of the information that is presented. In the preceding case, facts were omitted that perpetuated racist ways of knowing. In the case of the ABE students, facts were omitted that perpetuated sexist courses of action. In the current instance, theories that may only reflect the reality of one group of people were discussed as being relevant to all groups of people. The acknowledgement that certain theories have been based on a single population does nothing to provide more inclusive or alternative theories of development.

Institutional practices can be discriminatory. The tendency to depend on Graduate Record Examination (GRE) scores as predictors of an individual's performance in graduate school prevents the admission of many members of minority groups and women. Often, defenders of these policies believe that the degree awarded by the institution would diminish in quality if applicants did not perform well on standardized admission tests. There is now evidence that the GRE score is not necessarily predictive of success in graduate programs (Milner, McNeil, and King, 1984). But many adult educators continue to believe that the scores are reliable and retain their faith in the institutions that maintain them as admissions criteria. They often insist that the policy is enforced by the institution and that they have no role in the effect that it has on minorities and women. A different interpretation is that policies are not made by institutions but by persons in them who occupy positions of authority. The policies are expressions of prejudice, sanctioned not only by the administrators who make them but by those who conform to them.

## Why Racism and Sexism Persist in Adult Education

The examples in the preceding section were chosen to show how both racism and sexism can play out in our daily interactions with adult learners. Racism and sexism are usually hard to pinpoint. They are the most insidious and dangerous when they pass unnoticed in the practice of adult educators. Racism and sexism are perpetuated by the failure to see that an event can have differing interpretations; by the omission of facts or theories; by the assumption that theories based on male, white, middle-class populations are applicable to all populations; and by allowing discriminatory institutional practices to continue. This section contains some general observations about why racism and sexism continue to exist in adult education.

**Discrepancy Between Language and Behavior.** In the past decade, adult educators have often prided themselves on being "enablers" or on "empowering" students. Politically correct as these terms may be, they often were accompanied by unempowering, traditional behaviors. The implicit and explicit racist and sexist behaviors of adult educators are often not examined if nonsexist and nonracist language is used. The statement *We value diversity* is meaningless if we are not making an active attempt to rid our institutions of sexist and racist behaviors. Politically correct language does not replace positive action. As McGuire (1991, p. 6) has said, "We cannot teach about equality if we do not practice equality. We cannot teach about justice if we do not practice justice." Helping adult educators understand the discrepancy between their language and behavior is one priority for in-service education.

**Lack of Experience with and Sensitivity to Other Cultures.** Most adult educators reflect the white, middle-class culture and interpret their interactions with minority group members from their own cultural context. Adult educators often unknowingly perpetuate racism and sexism. They often serve as models of, as well as experts on, what happens only in white sections of small towns and in rural and suburban schools and businesses. According to Haberman (1987, p. 26), "They do not and cannot teach what they don't know." People gain sensitivity through meaningful contact with women and minorities. If adult educators have little or no contact with minorities and if they have not examined sexist modes of action, then their chances of integrating alternative views into staff development materials and activities are effectively limited. Learning to recognize cultural biases and learning to accept other cultures are areas for growth.

**Faith in Institutional Practice.** Many adult educators as well as most primary and secondary educators have extraordinary faith in institutions. They believe for the most part that institutional practices are well meaning and that the policies under which their institutions operate are not biased. Since institutionalized racism and sexism are often subtle and less blatant than individual acts, staff development should deal with the beliefs reflected by institutions as well as those expressed by individuals.

Prejudice, discrimination, and racism do not have to be intentional (Pine and Hilliard, 1990). The exclusion of many minority students from graduate programs may not be intentionally racist, but their exclusion is discriminatory. Many people believe that it is appropriate to act as though minority status makes no difference in program policies or individual interactions. However, as the filmmaker Spike Lee has said, "One of the biggest lies out here is that, no matter what race or religion you are, it doesn't matter. Now that's a lie, and we all know it. If we don't talk about these problems and take them on, they're going to get much, much worse" (Muwakkie, 1989, p. 13).

Institutional policies are sometimes purposefully designed to avoid issues of race and gender. Administrators claim that everyone has an equal chance and therefore that neither race nor gender are considered in program policies and guidelines. Such avoidance of the issues of race and gender helps to maintain the status quo, because it does not permit white women and members of minority groups to demonstrate their unique contributions and potentials. As Giddings (1990, p. 15) has noted, "If the institution could not deal with the encompassing notion of race, one had also to question the entire nature of reality as expressed in institutional life." If institutional practices do not acknowledge and value the diversity of all people, they are exclusionary. Attempts to change institutional policies often begin with either formal or informal staff development programs. Unfortunately, change usually involves confrontation and struggle.

For some minorities, the call for diversity from mainstream adult educators sounds like this: "Come on in, but don't change anything" (Minow, 1990, p. 24). The more an individual reflects an institution and its accompanying values, the more easily that person is accepted in its structure. In contrast, individuals who maintain their cultural heritage and bring different views to the institution are often not understood and not accepted. Through staff development, adult educators can help to make spaces for a variety of people and viewpoints.

## Strategies to Address Racism and Sexism

Effective staff development programs use a variety of strategies to encourage racial and gender equity. It is not the purpose of this chapter to specify how to conduct such programs. Rather, the emphasis here is on their content and on specific activities that may be helpful. Examining biases and reframing questions are two strategies that can be used in both formal and informal staff development programs.

**Examining Biases.** Our interactions with other adult educators and learners are an expression of who and what we value. For example, when teachers sit together at break only with other teachers or tutors, they confirm their distance from adult learners and silently reveal whom they value in the educational mainstream. The beliefs displayed are often more evident to learners than they are to adult educators, since the learners live under the impact of those beliefs. It is for this reason that, to be effective, staff development must encourage people to "step outside of the parochialism and ethnocentrism of believing that one's own culture's methods are most correct and be ready to see reality through the eyes of diverse cultures" (Hillis, 1991, p. 5).

Staff development should give adult educators ways to explore their own beliefs. If they are unwilling or unable to challenge their own assumptions, they are less likely to communicate effectively with persons from other cultures. If adult educators assume an allegedly neutral stance in all areas, they have effectively removed themselves from the realities of learners. Adult educators need to learn how to admit that they have biases. They should specify what they stand for but at the same time provide a nonthreatening forum for open dialogue. Values clarification activities should precede activities that promote the examination of our perceptions of interactions.

**Questioning.** One particularly useful way of encouraging people to accept diverse views is by helping them to frame questions in different ways. Staff development can help adult educators out of "accepted relationships by questioning the dominant/subordinate relationships to which they are accustomed" (Weiter, 1988, pp. 131–132). Here is one typical question: Why are women underrepresented in engineering, science, and math? This question compares women to a standard that men have set. Here is another question that could generate additional views: Why are men underrepresented in teaching, nursing, and child care? Asking a different question puts a new perspective on the same issue.

Here are some other questions that could generate discussion: Is what we do as adult educators mostly the result of convention and tradition? If so, have we excluded some people and viewpoints? Should we require students to work in multiracial, mixed-gender groups so that part of what they practice is working together in diverse groups? Guy-Sheftall (1991, p. 27) suggests other questions: "Can we teach in ways that don't reinforce structures of domination, racism, and sexism? How can we use our power as adult educators in ways that are not coercive, punitive, or controlling? Can we undo the 'miseducation' that most students have been subjected to by the time they enter our adult education classes? Can we undo our own 'miseducation,' since most of us are also victims of patriarchal, racist, sexist ways of knowing and teaching?"

## Formal Staff Development Programs

Formal programs of staff development are usually based on content identified through a needs assessment, facilitated by an adult educator, delivered by an institution, and evaluated for short-term effectiveness. This section on formal programs examines the content that could be used to address race and gender issues.

Sexism and racism cannot be eliminated in a day or a week as a result of one or two workshops. There is evidence that courses designed to help individuals understand the cultures of various groups tend to be largely descriptive and informational, "providing teachers with generalizations about group characteristics and customs. This information can inadvertently reinforce, rather than alter, latent prejudices" (Kennedy, 1991, p. 15). Workshops and staff development activities that attempt to teach someone how to deal, for example, with Hispanic students are often detrimental to individuals. Generalizations, such as *Native Americans tend to be more collaborative than competitive*, may be true for one individual or group but not for another. If staff development aimed at fostering multicultural understanding uses generalizations about minority groups, it can reinforce existing prejudices, since generalizations often become stereotypes.

Formal "diversity" programs give cause for other concerns. For example, if the workshop topic appears to be peripheral to the primary goal of the institution, participants often do not view it as integral to what teachers do. The pedagogical implications of learners' diversity are usually not clear. Adult educators also may assume that knowledge of student diversity is not relevant to their particular program area, so they may not recognize its importance to their own activities. Formal programs on multiculturalism sometimes lull individuals into thinking that racial and gender issues have been addressed through specific workshops. Consequently, they feel no need to deal with the real issues.

Nevertheless, formal workshops and seminars have a role to play in the struggle against racism and sexism. Workshops can stimulate awareness, which must be raised if behavior is to be changed. Diversity and its implications are priorities that require ongoing attention in a staff development program. To enhance participation and promote discussion of issues about which some individuals may be sensitive, relatively small groups of between ten and twelve members are recommended.

**Goals.** Formal programs related to issues of gender and race need to have specific goals. One model for the goals that such workshops can have is provided by the Intercultural Communication Workshops (ICWs) that were initiated at the University of Pittsburgh. Instead of abstract goals, such as gaining an understanding and appreciation of different cultures, the ICWs had three very specific goals: To increase the participant's ability to identify the cultural dimensions of verbal and nonverbal behavior and his or her other learned characteristics; to increase the participant's ability to identify the cultural dimensions of verbal and nonverbal behavior and other learned characteristics of persons from other cultures; and to increase the participant's ability to identify areas in which differences cause difficulty in communicating interpersonally with persons of other cultures (Harris and Moran, 1987).

Colin and Preciphs (1991) suggested that a reasonable way of helping adult educators to change their perceptions was to foster critical self-reflection. Their recommendations for confronting racism included the goal of eradicating "distorted perceptions" by "sensitizing individuals to how perceptions are formed and become distorted" (p. 67). This goal required "acknowledgement by adult education practitioners that racism exists and commitment by adult education practitioners to address racism in the learning environment" (p. 66).

Once the goals have been specified, the staff development program must tie them to the daily activities of staff. For adult basic education teachers, the goals need to relate to improving student learning. Understanding the racial and gender issues surrounding instruction should improve student–teacher communication. Improving communication between them should in turn result in improved learning. In human resource development programs, the goals need to be connected to increasing productivity or other business activities. If the program offers proposes to help participants understand cultural diversity but it is not relevant to their work environment, it is often not perceived as necessary, and the information conveyed will probably be forgotten or ignored.

**Content.** The content of these seminars can include definitions and types of diversity, examinations of communication skills, and explorations of diverse cultures. It is crucial for the terms *diversity* and *multicultural* to be defined so broadly that they include everyone. These terms are often applied to the perspectives of minority groups, females, and other groups whose norms are not white, Eurocentric, or male. Applying these terms in this way often leads white males to be excluded or to be blamed for existing conditions. White men can feel resentful if they do not feel included in the dialogue. White culture has many components, each with its own characteristics. If white, middle-class male culture is included in the definition of diversity, then the strengths and unique characteristics of every culture can be valued (Gordon, 1992).

Topics for discussion can include family life and the norms, beliefs, and types of communication within families in various cultures. Concepts of work and play in diverse cultures, male-female relationships (either cross-culturally or in a single culture), and the relationship between language and culture can also be themes. Other possible topics include concepts of competition, friendship, intimacy, and value orientations (task versus relationship, sense of time) (Ploumis-Devick, 1992).

Another way of organizing content is to design activities within a framework suggested by Mills (1986, p. 45): "Affective domain experiences . . . cultivate the attitudes of acceptance and respect for worth, dignity, and integrity of various groups and individuals. Cognitive domain experiences . . . expand knowledge and understanding of various ethnic groups and culturally diverse individuals, including the explicit and implicit characteristics of their lifeways. Interpersonal interactions [and] experiences . . . develop skill in communication and behaving appropriately with the culturally diverse." General topics need to be applied to specific issues at the local level. Speaking in generalities does nothing to change the behavior of individuals or institutions.

**Packaged Programs.** Many schools and businesses use consultants or packaged programs to increase multicultural sensitivity. The advantage of consultants and packaged programs is that they can provide an introduction to and overview of the process. Media programs are usually of high visual quality. When there are no internal facilitators or resources in the community, packaged programs can be helpful.

However, packaged programs have several disadvantages. First, they do not address specific local issues. Second, if they contain many generalizations about specific groups, they may perpetuate stereotypes that are not helpful when participants must deal with individual learners. Third, the consultant or program provider has no responsibility or ongoing relationship with staff after the activity, which limits the chances that staff will be affected permanently by the in-service.

## Informal Staff Development Activities

Informal staff development is a practical approach whose activities reside outside a formal program of workshops and seminars. It often lets teachers assume responsibility for their own staff development. Staff development facilitators should explain the philosophy or rationale for informal activities. Expectations for participation need to be developed with learner input. It is helpful if the program staff emphasize the nonjudgmental approach in the program. As Pine and Hilliard (1990, p. 597) put it, "staff development programs should be designed not to put people on the defensive but to empower them to under-stand and address the unconscious and overt effects of the institutional racism that pervades all facets of society."

Development of nonracist and nonsexist behaviors should be explored in a collaborative manner. Through these informal experiences, staff development managers can expect differential growth. Individuals do not examine issues of race and gender or make internal adjustments on a standardized, linear scale. For some people, one insight may result in a huge adjustment of behavior. For others, consistent reflection and acquired experience may lead slowly to changes in behavior that take place over months and years.

**Mentoring and Peer Coaching.** One-to-one interaction can be a potent staff development tool. Through mentoring or peer coaching, a person can demonstrate ways of speaking and behaving that discourage racist and sexist behavior by staff, students, or both. This approach is particularly useful if employees do not recognize that they play a role in the perpetuation of preju-dice. For example, if a staff member refers to a group of female secretaries as "the girls," it may be helpful to have another trusted individual immediately and confidentially explain why some people view that phrase as sexist. Men-toring and peer coaching are particularly helpful when content goes beyond technical skills. Mentoring and coaching are effective when learning "involves choices of a personal, moral, and sociopolitical nature" (Hargreaves and Dawe, 1989, p. 20). Obviously, those selected to be mentors must reflect racial and gender equity in their own behaviors and language.

**Experiences in Other Cultural Settings.** The objective of staff develop-ment that places participants in other cultural settings is to sensitize them to people who live in very different circumstances. The Community Internship Program implemented by the United Parcel Service more than twenty-five years ago illustrates this approach. As Filipczak (1992, p. 42) explains, "The rationale . . . is simple. Being aware of an issue is not the same as knowing about it, and knowing about it is not the same as doing something about it." Through placements at community service organizations, staff development programs can help individuals to view society from a different perspective. For English-as-a-second-language teachers, spending two weeks in a legal aid office that specializes in immigration issues can give participants new perspectives on the lives of their students. A male employee can attend activities at a local chapter of the National Organization of Women to gain insight into gender issues. Providing adult educators with release time to participate in cross-cultural experiences can be seen as an integral component of a staff develop-ment program that seeks to sensitize personnel to diversity issues.

**Critical Self-Reflection.** To change perceptions and beliefs and the behaviors that result from them, critical self-reflection can be an effective form of staff development. The insights gained can give participants the background and motivation they need to challenge accepted practices and assumptions. While this type of staff development can be the most difficult to implement, it also has the potential to have significant impact. It needs to be individualized, with a course of action proposed by the person who wants to undertake reflective activities.

The role for a staff developer who wants to encourage critical self-reflection includes providing the learner with options, identifying resources and facilitating the learner's use of them, and encouraging activities that help individuals to give voice to their changing perceptions. Learners may need assistance in identifying options. Suggest visits to libraries and museums that feature artifacts from various cultures. Make available reading materials, including fiction and nonfiction works, that illustrate the lived experience of racism and sexism. Give participants opportunities for informal discussion and interaction with women and people of color. Provide staff with questions as a starting point for their reflection. Encourage learners to use journals and diaries to record their perceptions and track their changing perceptions over time.

## Cautions and Challenges

The literature on staff development has acknowledged that adults learn best when activities are based on real experiences (Brookfield, 1986; Knowles, 1980) and have careful and continuous guided reflection (Mezirow and Associates, 1990; Schön, 1983). There must also be continuity and reinforcement, challenge and support. These supports are vital with the often sensitive issues of race and gender.

The old adage, "Do what you can, where you are, with what you've got," is appropriate in many staff development situations. Appreciating diversity cannot wait until the time is right and all conditions are perfect. It must begin now, with the resources that are currently available. Since changing behavior and attitudes are long-term objectives, do not expect success overnight. Strive for small gains, which cumulatively will begin to change the atmosphere in your program. James Freedman, president of Dartmouth College, perhaps put it most succinctly: "Diversity takes time to achieve. It's not a course of action for the fainthearted. It's a course of action for those who are here for the long-term" (McLaughlin, 1991, p. 31).

As staff development begins to address issues of language, lack of experience, and lack of sensitivity and to challenge the prevailing faith in institutional behaviors, a more accurate picture of the racism and sexism in institutional life will emerge. Formal activities can be offered that relate to the goals of your adult education program. The resulting seminars and workshops should be

paired with informal staff development activities, such as mentoring, intern-
ships, and self-reflection.

Issues of race and gender should be addressed holistically. Overcoming
one wrong while allowing others to persist is contrary to the goal of appreciating diversity. Let adult educators commit to diversity now by promoting
appropriate staff development activities.

## References

*American Heritage Dictionary.* New York: Dell, 1983.

Brookfield, S. D. *Understanding and Facilitating Adult Learning: A Comprehensive Analysis of Principles and Effective Practices.* San Francisco: Jossey-Bass, 1986.

Colin, S.A.J., III, and Preciphs, T. "Perceptual Patterns and the Learning Environment: Confronting
White Racism." In R. Hiemstra (ed.), *Creating Environments for Effective Adult Learning.* New
Directions for Adult and Continuing Education, no. 50. San Francisco: Jossey-Bass, 1991.

Filipczak, B. "Twenty-Five Years of Diversity at UPS." *Training,* 1992, *29* (8), 42–45.

Giddings, P. "Education, Race, and Reality: A Legacy of the 60s." *Change,* 1990, 22 (2), 15–17.

Gollnick, D. "Understanding the Dynamics of Race, Class, and Gender." In M. E. Dilworth (ed.),
*Diversity in Teacher Education: New Expectations.* San Francisco: Jossey-Bass, 1992.

Gordon, J. "Rethinking Diversity." *Training,* 1992, *29* (1), 23–30.

Guy-Sheftall, B. "Practicing What You Preach: Strategies of an Ex-English Professor." *Liberal Education,* 1991, 77 (1), 27–29.

Haberman, M. *Recruiting and Selecting Teachers for Urban Schools.* ERIC/CUE Urban Diversity
Series, no. 95. New York: ERIC Clearinghouse on Urban Education, 1987.

Hargreaves, A., and Dawe, R. "Coaching as Unreflective Practice: Contrived Collegiality or Collaborative Culture?" Paper presented at the annual meeting of the American Educational
Research Association, San Francisco, Nov. 6, 1989.

Harris, P., and Moran, R. *Managing Cultural Differences.* (2nd ed.) Houston: Gulf Publishing,
1987.

Hillis, R. "Counseling Across Cultures: Collaboration Between Family, School, and Community."
Paper presented at the 99th annual convention of the American Psychological Association, San
Francisco, Aug. 16, 1991.

Jackson, P. W. "Old Dogs and New Tricks: Observations on the Continuing Education of Teachers." In L. J. Rubin (ed.), *Improving In-Service Education: Proposals and Procedures for Change.*
Boston: Allyn & Bacon, 1971.

Kennedy, M. "Some Surprising Findings on How Teachers Learn to Teach." *Educational Leadership,* 1991, *49* (3), 14–17.

Knowles, M. *The Modern Practice of Adult Education: From Pedagogy to Andragogy.* Englewood
Cliffs, N.J.: Prentice Hall, 1980.

McGuire, P. "Perspectives on Multiculturalism and Political Correctness." *Liberal Education,* 1991,
77 (4), 2–11.

McLaughlin, J. B. "James O. Freedman on Diversity and Dartmouth." *Change,* 1991, 23 (5), 25–31.

Mezirow, J., and Associates. *Fostering Critical Reflection in Adulthood: A Guide to Transformative
and Emancipatory Learning.* San Francisco: Jossey-Bass, 1990.

Mills, J. R. *Cross-Cultural Conflict in Higher Education.* Boone, N.C.: National Association for Developmental Education, 1986.

Milner, M., McNeil, J., and King, W. "The GRE: A Question of Validity in Predicting Performance
in Professional Schools of Social Work." *Educational and Psychological Measurement,* 1984,
44 (4), 945–950.

Minow, M. "On Neutrality, Equality, and Tolerance: New Norms for a Decade of Distinction."
*Change,* 1990, 22 (1), 17–25.

Muwakkie, S. "Doing the Spike Thing." *In These Times*, July 5–18, 1989, pp. 13, 29.

Orlich, D. *Staff Development: Enhancing Human Potential*. Boston: Allyn & Bacon, 1987.

Pine, G., and Hilliard, A. "Rx for Racism: Imperatives for America's Schools. *Phi Delta Kappan*, 1990, 71 (8), 593–600.

Ploumis-Devick, E. *Appreciating Differences: Teaching and Learning in a Culturally Diverse Classroom*. Greensboro, N.C.: Southeastern Regional Vision for Education, University of North Carolina at Greensboro, and Florida Department of Education, 1992.

Schön, D. A. *The Reflective Practitioner*. New York: Basic Books, 1983.

Weiler, K. *Women Teaching for Change*. South Hadley, Mass.: Bergvin and Garvey, 1988.

*DONNA D. AMSTUTZ, who has more than eighteen years of experience in staff development, is assistant professor of adult education at the University of Wyoming and director of the Wyoming Literacy Resource Center.*

# Adult and Continuing Education Graduate Programs: Prescription for the Future

*Scipio A. J. Colin III*

> The Supreme Court decision of 1954 made discrimination based on color illegal. It did not make racism illegal. The basic problem was then and is now the inability or unwillingness of the institution to adapt its infrastructure to meet the reasonable needs of black and minority students and faculty.
>
> —C. A. Fields (1988, p. 48)

The current groundswell of concern and criticism regarding the role of adult and continuing education in the perpetuation of racial, cultural, and gender bias has focused in particular on the content and composition of our graduate programs. This chapter focuses on racism in adult continuing education graduate programs: the recruitment and retention of African Ameripean[1] faculty and students and the exclusion of the Africentric[2] perspective from curriculum content. To answer the question, How can we eliminate the racial and cultural bias reflected in our curriculum? the appendix to this chapter provides a list of literature that reflects the Africentric perspective on the foundations of adult education and theories of adult learning and development. A list of organizational resources is also included.

The issues of exclusion raised in this chapter are in no way limited to African Ameripeans, for similar observations and conclusions can be reached as a result of comparative analyses of bias against Native Americans, Hispanic Americans, and women.

NEW DIRECTIONS FOR ADULT AND CONTINUING EDUCATION, no. 61, Spring 1994 © Jossey-Bass Publishers

## Faculty Perceptions and Responsibilities

In view of the sociodemographic changes projected for the twenty-first cen-
tury, if we are to fulfill our mission as I perceive it, then the professoriat must
become more knowledgeable about the cultural milieu of the racial groups that
comprise this society. Graduate faculty must begin by acknowledging that
racism seriously affects the lives of America's nonwhite populations. They must
be willing to confront their personal racism and acknowledge the impact that
it has on their practice and perceptions of nonwhite groups. This self-reflection will not necessitate a change in the general purpose of our programs, but
it will help us to accomplish our goals and influence the way in which we
recruit faculty and students and develop our courses. Eurocentric norms and
perceptions dominate the academic environment, and this dominance is
reflected in the criteria that are used for hiring and admissions. Academia
judges people of color by Euroamerican standards. By imposing such standards, the professoriat exercises its power to exclude. This power is based on
deeply ingrained attitudes and perceptions that are the result of prior miseducation, stereotypes, and myths of racial superiority and inferiority (Colin and
Preciphs, 1991; Harvey, in press; Washington and Harvey, 1989).

I have raised the issue of racism in the curricula of adult and continuing
education graduate programs at the past three annual meetings of the Commission of Professors of Adult Education (CPAE). Its membership has as its primary responsibilities the creation of a knowledge base, the formal education
of practitioners and future professors, the development of curricula, and the
recruitment and retention of faculty and students. Accordingly, the members
of the professoriat were encouraged to reflect on the attitudes and perceptions
regarding traditionally excluded groups—specifically African Ameripeans—
and to determine the extent to which racist assumptions frame their policies,
practices, and programs. Clearly, faculty are responsible for the creation and
maintenance of a nurturing and positive learning environment for students and
of a collegial environment for faculty. The professoriat plays an important role
regarding the success or failure of faculty members, for their recruitment and
retention are predicated on perceptions of their abilities. Thus far, most faculty
in adult and continuing education have refused to acknowledge that their perceptions and practices are racist or to accept responsibility for the perpetuation of racism. The professoriat is again being challenged regarding the
Eurocentric nature of its curricula and the validity of the assumptions that
frame policies on the recruitment and retention of African Ameripean faculty
and students.

## Recruitment of African Ameripeans

The matriculation of African Ameripean students tends to be predicated on the
degree of their commitment to the Eurocentric worldview, value system, and

modes of behavior. And the tenure and promotion of African Ameripean faculty tend to be based on the level of their commitment to the perpetuation of this ideology in the classroom and their own research. As such, African Ameripean faculty are expected to trade their cultural reality for reappointment and truth for tenure (Colin, 1990; Harvey, in press).

It is mistakenly assumed that these faculty members and students are there because of affirmative action, an assumption that equates color with competence, and that they are the beneficiaries of acts of favoritism. Nothing could be farther from the truth. If anything, they are treated with disdain, and they become the targets of acts of overt and covert racism, which have been extensively documented (Harvey, 1987, in press; Harvey and Scott-Jones, 1985; Moses, 1989; Scott-Jones and Harvey, 1985; Washington and Harvey, 1989; Wilson, 1987). One must keep in mind that their mere presence in the arena of higher education seriously challenges the myth that the members of this group are intellectually inferior.

**Issues for Faculty.** The perceived quality and appropriateness of research focused on African Ameripean concerns and reflecting the Africentric perspective are issues that both faculty and students confront. Although those who reject African Ameripean concerns in the name of objectivity state that the issue is one of appropriate methodology, the issue really involves the purpose and focus of research and the use of an Africentric frame of analysis (Colin, 1991b). As one authority (Harvey, in press, p. 7) states, "Issues that directly affect their [African Ameripeans'] lives, their communities, and their futures are likely to be considered inappropriate research topics, though the situation seems to be the reverse for their white counterparts." This issue is complicated for the faculty member, because promotion and tenure decisions are based on the number of publications in refereed journals. The requirement to publish in refereed journals raises two problems for the African Ameripean professor: what the field has designated as refereed and the double standard regarding manuscript acceptance.

For example, *Adult Education Quarterly* is widely recognized as a refereed journal, but the *Journal of Negro Education* (established in 1932) and the *Journal of Negro History* (established in 1916) are not, although they are in fact refereed and although they predate journals that the field now considers to be primary. Although our literature and our curricula reference articles published in mainstream publications, one would be hard pressed to find references to the information included in the special 1945 issue of the *Journal of Negro Education* titled "Adult Education and the Negro." This lack of awareness and devaluation of culturally grounded publications reflect the Eurocentric view of the world and limit publication opportunities for African Ameripean faculty whose research focuses on African Ameripean concerns.

The double standard for manuscript acceptance is exemplified by the requirement that a selected historical overview of African Ameripean adult education must be "grounded in theory," whereas the manuscripts that focus on mainstream adult education activities need only to document that these activities occurred.

**Issues for Graduate Students.** There are two prevailing myths regarding African Ameripean students: First, qualified students cannot be found. Second, these students are not intellectually equipped for the rigors of graduate studies. This attitude is reflected in the argument that the degree will be cheapened and questions will be raised about admission standards and about the quality and rigor of the program if too many are admitted. The assumptions underlying these professed concerns, whether we choose to admit it or not, are based on the racist myth that the members of this racial group do not possess the intellectual abilities that are required to think critically and conduct quality research (Colin and Preciphs, 1991, Colin, 1991b; Harvey, 1993; Melvaux, 1993; Moses, 1989; Phillip, 1993; Peterson, 1991; Wheeler, 1992). Admissions criteria, such as GRE scores, may be used to support these assumptions and perpetuate the exclusion of African Ameripean students. The possibility that such criteria may be racially and culturally biased is not given serious consideration.

The myths and perceptions regarding the African Ameripean's intellectual abilities and the expectation of failure are distinctively different from the perceptions and expectations held by the faculty at historical black colleges and universities. They, unlike some members of our professoriat, assume that African Ameripean students have the intellectual capabilities and potential to engage in critical thinking and analysis. Their students are successful in the very kind of intellectual endeavors that are expected of students in our adult and continuing education graduate programs. There is much that can be learned from our colleagues at these institutions about the positive aspect of the self-fulfilling prophecy and the process of creating and maintaining a supportive teaching-learning environment.

The perceptions, problems, and obstacles that graduate student researchers confront are not unlike those experienced by their faculty counterparts (Colin, 1991b; Peterson, 1991; Harvey, 1993; Moses, 1989). As one study (Moses, 1989, p. 4) has shown, African Ameripean graduate students "whose research focuses on issues of particular concern to [them] may be dismissed, devalued, or not enthusiastically supported." Clearly, faculty confront similar problems.

All students should be required to know, understand, analyze, and articulate the philosophies, theories, and adult education activities of African Ameripeans (Colin, 1991b). The following questions might be used to identify deficiencies and possible topics of research: Are you able to discuss the implications for curricula of Locke's (1918) theory of value? Do you know the purposes, activities, or curricula of such culturally grounded organizations as the National Association of Colored Women, the Universal Negro Improvement Association—African Communities League, or African Ameripean religious denominations? Does your research focus on some aspect of the African Ameripean experience? If so, does the content reflect the culturally grounded

Africentric literature base? How much do you know about emancipatory social transformation? (Colin, 1991a, 1991b).

## Curricula

Our field will suffer or flourish, depending on practitioner preparation. If our course content does not reflect the sociocultural and intellectual bodies of knowledge representative of various racial, ethnic, and gender groups, how well we are preparing our students to function in the real world? Graduate study should enable our students to challenge the validity of prevailing assumptions and theories. It should not be a process of memorization and regurgitation of Eurocentric ideology. One way to facilitate the process of critical thinking is to include diverse perspectives and competing bodies of knowledge. Our responsibility, as I see it, is to awaken and facilitate in our students an inquisitive approach to content and subsequent conclusions of systematic inquiry that ask not merely what is there but what is not there.

Thus far, our graduate programs serve only to reinforce the Eurocentric perspective. They are transmitters of cultures and disseminators of knowledge. We must expand our frames of reference and interpretation and question the exclusiveness of the Eurocentric view that frames our programs and therefore our practice. One of the guiding principles that we teach is that learning is lifelong and that it involves self-reflection and perspective change. Accordingly, it is incumbent on members of the professoriat to practice what it teaches.

Our graduate programs should have as their primary goal giving all students an opportunity to understand the diversity of life experiences and sociocultural and intellectual histories. The curricula must be based on an analysis and synthesis of all available literature. The inclusion of the contributions of others would expand the knowledge base, influencing not only what is taught in the classroom but also the type and content of the adult and continuing education programs that are being offered to African Ameripeans. The following sections provide examples of Africentric literature on the foundations of adult education and theories of adult learning and development.

**Foundations.** The courses that focus on intellectual and institutional development should include the activities and thinking of African Ameripeans, including Alain Locke (1918) and Ambrose Caliver (1939). Although they were the first two African Ameripean presidents of the American Association for Adult Education, one would be hard pressed to find them mentioned in the writings and discussions of the association. Although both men produced numerous works relative to the field, their works are not included in the courses that focus on the philosophical and ideological aspects of the field, nor are there a significant number of professors who know anything about them (Colin, 1988).

Moreover, many of our graduate students are introduced to the Frankfurt school of critical theory through the works of Horkheimer, Adorno, and

Habermas, among others. The contributions of the Howard University school of critical thinking and the works of Locke, Holmes, McAllister, and others are ignored. Whether one classifies these African Ameripean philosophers as pragmatists, Pan-Africanists, racialists, or moral suasionists, they must be read. Our students should be as familiar with Africentric theoretical constructs and philosophical formulations as they are with those reflecting the Eurocentric worldview.

**Adult Learning and Development.**  In our adult learning and development courses, we teach life cycle and life-span developmental models, but we ignore the models that focus on African Ameripean adult development in the context of racist society (Cross, 1971, 1978; DuBois, [1903] 1969; Parham, 1989; Thomas, 1971). These models are the result of research that reflects the Africentric perspective in its focus on the development of the racial self and the bond between the individual and the racial group and the impact that racist interactions have on the development of the self-ethnic image (Colin, 1989, 1991b).

Regarding the literature on adult development, one authority (Jones, 1989, p. xi) observed that "there is little attention to black adults as subjects of investigation, the one exception being the black elderly . . . Research and studies on black early and middle adulthood, however, are rare. [Such topics] as the impact of race, the culture of racism, cohort differences related to race, [and] racial identity development—all areas critical to an understanding of black adult development—received no attention in these books."

By not preparing our students adequately, we are in conflict with our mission and working against our own best interest. We are the professoriat turning out professionals. Therefore, we should bear in mind a theorem of physics: An object can be no greater than its source. The implication of this theorem is that our practice can be no more inclusive than the ideas on which it is based.

## Recommendations

The following recommendations can serve as a starting point for additional efforts to overcome racism in adult education graduate programs.

• The CPAE should offer sessions focused on faculty and student recruitment and retention strategies and curriculum development at its national meeting.

• Faculty and university officials should work with African Ameripean students and sponsor seminars, workshops, and forums that focus on issues and areas of interest relevant to them. The symposiums sponsored by the Adult Continuing Education Black Graduate Students Association at Northern Illinois University are an example of what can be done.

• Faculty and university officials should establish linkages with the historically black colleges and universities. Such linkages will stimulate an interest in the field and help to develop a pool of potential students. A collaborative relationship could also result in the creation of adult education prep programs similar to the tech prep programs that link high schools with community colleges. To facilitate this linkage, a collaborative relationship should be established with the United Negro College Fund's national office.

• The members of the professoriat should review their course content and become as familiar with culturally grounded literature as they already are with the mainstream literature. They should review and include in their course readings appropriate literature from such publications as the *Black Scholar*, the *Journal of Black Psychology*, the *Western Journal of Black Studies*, *Black Issues in Higher Education*, the *Journal of Negro Education*, and the *Journal of Negro History*.

## Conclusion

Before we can confront the issue of societal racism, members of the professoriat must first confront the racism that is reflected in their perceptions of and attitudes toward people of color and determine how this racism is acted out in their recruitment and retention practices. The impact of racism on the participation of African Ameripean graduate students has been addressed elsewhere (Colin, 1989, 1991b) as has the impact of practitioners' racist perceptual patterns on the teaching-learning environment (Colin and Preciphs, 1991). Now we must focus on the two sacred cows of our field: the professoriat and our graduate curricula.

Our curricula must incorporate knowledge that comes from outside the Eurocentric, dominant cultural and ideological framework. Inclusion of such knowledge would have a positive impact on the recruitment and retention of African Ameripean faculty and students. By including this knowledge base, we make space for those current and potential research scholars who possess such knowledge and who have an Africentric perspective.

Acceptance of the Eurocentric worldview excludes the sociocultural and intellectual histories and life experiences of African Ameripeans. It physically and cognitively locks them out, but it locks others in. If we are to meet the needs of all members of the society whom we as adult educators are to serve, we must become inclusive in theory and practice. Given the racial and cultural diversity of American society, adult and continuing education graduate programs can no longer rely on the Eurocentric approach to recruitment, retention, and curricula development.

## Appendix

The print resources described in this appendix were selected from a bibliography of African Ameripean adult education that includes more than 500 items that focus on curricula, foundations, history and philosophy, the psychology of adult learning and development, and individuals and organizations from the 1600s to the present (Colin, 1993). To facilitate the reader's search, the list reflects resources that are readily available. A list of organizations concludes the appendix.

## History

Butchart, R. E. *Northern Schools, Southern Blacks, and Reconstruction: Freedmen's Education, 1862–1875.* Westport, Conn.: Greenwood Press, 1980.

Cornelius, J. D. *When I Can Read My Title Clear: Literacy, Slavery, and Religion in the Antebellum South.* Columbia: University of South Carolina Press, 1991.

McGee, L., and Neufeldt, H. G. *Education of the Black Adult in the United States: An Annotated Bibliography.* Westport, Conn.: Greenwood Press, 1985.

Neufeldt, H. G., and McGee, L. (eds.). *Education of the African American Adult: An Historical Overview.* Westport, Conn.: Greenwood Press, 1990.

Spivey, D. *Schooling for the New Slavery: Black Industrial Education 1865–1915.* Westport, Conn.: Greenwood Press, 1978.

Wilkins, T. B. "Ambrose Caliver: Distinguished Civil Servant." *Journal of Negro Education,* 1962, *31,* 212–214.

Woodson, C. G. *Education of the Negro Prior to 1861.* New York: Arno Press, 1968. (Originally published 1915.)

## Philosophy

Asante, M. K. *The Afrocentric Idea.* Philadelphia: Temple University Press, 1987.

Harris, L. (ed.). *Philosophy Born of Struggle: Anthology of Afro-American Philosophy from 1917.* Dubuque, Iowa: Kendall/Hunt, 1983.

Moiti, J. S. *African Religions and Philosophies.* Garden City, N.Y.: Anchor Books, 1970.

Washington, J. *Alain Locke and Philosophy: A Quest for Cultural Pluralism.* Westport, Conn.: Greenwood Press, 1986.

## Adult Learning and Development

Harel, Z., McKinney, E. A., and Williams, M. *Black Aged.* Newbury Park, Calif.: Sage, 1990.

Jackson, J. S., Chatters, L. M., and Taylor, R. J. (eds.). *Aging in Black America.* Newbury Park, Calif.: Sage, 1992.

Jenkins, A. *The Psychology of the Afro-American.* New York: Pergamon Press, 1982.

Parham, T. A. "Nigrescence: The Transformation of Black Consciousness Across the Life Cycle." In R. L. Jones (ed.), *Black Adult Development and Aging.* Berkeley, Calif.: Cobb and Henry Publishers, 1989.

## Organizations

Association of Black Psychologists, c/o Dr. Craig C. Brookins, Department of Psychology, Box 7801, North Carolina State University, Raleigh, NC 27695–7801.

Black Caucus of American Association for Higher Education, One Dupont Circle, Suite 600, Washington, DC 20030.
National Alliance of African Ameripean Adult Educators, c/o Dr. Scipio A. J. Colin III, Department of Adult and Community College Education, Box 7801, North Carolina State University, Raleigh, NC 27695–7801.
National Association for Equal Opportunity in Higher Education, Lovejoy Building, 400 12th Street, N.E., Washington, DC 20002.
National Black Graduate Student Association (Phelps Foundation), 1100 92nd Street, New York, NY 10018.
National Congress of Black Faculty, c/o Dr. Ronald Waters, Howard University, 2400 6th Street, N.W., Washington, DC 20059.
United Negro College Fund, 500 East 62nd Street, New York, NY 10021.

## Notes

1. See Editors' Notes for a discussion of the use of the term *African Ameripean*.
2. The use of the terms *Africentric* and *Africentrism* is explained in the Editors' Notes.

## References

Caliver, A. "Adult Education of Negroes." *School Life,* 1939, 31–37.
Colin, S.A.J., III. "Voices from Beyond the Veil: Marcus Garvey, the Universal Negro Improvement Association, and the Education of African Ameripean Adults." Unpublished doctoral dissertation, Northern Illinois University, 1988.
Colin, S.A.J., III. "Cultural Literacy: Ethnocentrism Versus Self-Ethnic Reflectors." *Thresholds in Education,* 1989, *15* (4), 16–19.
Colin, S.A.J., III. "The Mission of the Commission of Professors." Paper presented at the annual meeting of the Commission of Professors of Adult Education, American Association for Adult and Continuing Education, Salt Lake City, Utah, Oct. 28, 1990.
Colin, S.A.J., III. "Voices from Beyond the Veil, Part II." Paper presented at the annual meeting of the Commission of Professors of Adult Education, American Association for Adult and Continuing Education, Montreal, Canada, Oct. 14, 1991a.
Colin, S.A.J., III. "African Ameripean Scholars and Scholarship: Who Will Bell the Cat?" In *Proceedings of the First Black Graduate Student Symposium in Adult Education.* De Kalb: Northern Illinois University, 1991b.
Colin, S.A.J., III. *African Ameripean Adult Education, 1619–Present: A Bibliography.* Unpublished manuscript (revised). North Carolina State University, Raleigh, 1993.
Colin, S.A.J., III, and Preciphs, T. K. "Perceptual Patterns and the Learning Environment: Confronting White Racism." In R. Hiemstra (ed.), *Creating Environments for Effective Adult Learning.* New Directions for Adult and Continuing Education, no. 50. San Francisco: Jossey-Bass, 1991.
Cross, W. E. "The Negro to Black Conversion Experience: Toward a Psychology of Black Liberation." *Black World,* 1971, *20* (9), 13–27.
Cross, W. E. "The Cross and Thomas Models of Psychological Nigrescence." *Journal of Black Psychology,* 1978, *5* (1), 13–19.
DuBois, W. E. B. *The Souls of Black Folk.* New York: New American Library, 1969. (Originally published 1903.)
Fields, C. A. "Institutional Responsibility and Minority Students." *Black Issues in Higher Education,* 1988, *5* (11), 48.
Harvey, W. B. "An Ebony View of the Ivory Tower." *Change,* 1987, *10,* 46–48.

Harvey, W. B. "Why African American Students Are Protesting." *Black Issues in Higher Education*, 1993, *9* (26), 96.

Harvey, W. B. "The Struggle That Faces African American Faculty in Predominately White Colleges and Universities." In L. See (ed.), *Terrorism in Academia: Black Professors Under Siege*. In press.

Harvey, W. B., and Scott-Jones, D. "We Can't Find Any: The Elusiveness of Black Faculty Members in American Higher Education." *Issues in Education*, 1985, *3*, 68–76.

Jones, R. L. (ed.). *Black Adult Development and Aging*. Berkeley, Calif.: Cobb and Henry Publishers, 1989.

Locke, A. L. "The Problems of Classification in the Theory of Value." Unpublished doctoral dissertation, Harvard University, 1918.

Malveaux, J. "Good Intentions Aren't Good Enough." *Black Issues in Higher Education*, 1993, *9* (24), 51.

Moses, Y. T. *Black Women in Academe: Issues and Strategies*. Washington, D.C.: Project on the Status and Education of Women, Association of American Colleges, 1989.

Parham, T. A. "Nigrescence: The Transformation of Black Consciousness Across the Life Cycle." In R. L. Jones (ed.), *Black Adult Development and Aging*. Berkeley, Calif.: Cobb and Henry Publishers, 1989.

Peterson, E. "Dispelling the Myths Confronting African American Academics." In *Proceedings of the First Black Graduate Student Symposium in Adult Education*. De Kalb: Northern Illinois University, 1991.

Phillip, M. C. "Too Many Institutions Still Taking Band-Aid Approach to Minority Student Retention, Experts Say." *Black Issues in Higher Education*, 1993, *9* (24), 24–26, 28.

Scott-Jones, D., and Harvey, W. B. "Hiring and Promoting Black Faculty." *Academe*, 1985, *71*, 37.

Thomas, C. *Boys No More*. Beverly Hills, Calif.: Glenco Press, 1971.

Washington, V., and Harvey, W. B. *Affirmative Rhetoric, Negative Action: African American and Hispanic Faculty at Predominately White Universities*. ASHE-ERIC Higher Education Report. Washington, D.C.: George Washington University, 1989.

Wheeler, P. H. "Fallacies About Recruiting and Retaining People of Color into Doctoral Programs of Study." *Black Issues in Higher Education*, 1992, *9* (10), 96.

Wilson, R. "Recruitment and Retention of Minority Faculty and Staff." *AAHE Bulletin*, 1987, *39* (6), 11–14.

*SCIPIO A. J. COLIN III is assistant professor of adult and continuing education at North Carolina State University, Raleigh.*

*Societal patterns of racism and sexism are played out in the professionalization of adult education.*

# Race, Gender, and the Politics of Professionalization

*Juanita Johnson Bailey, Elizabeth J. Tisdell, Ronald M. Cervero*

The professionalization of adult and continuing education is taking place in a society in which social power is distributed along many dimensions. A recognition of such a power distribution is essential for understanding why and how the power relationships in the professionalization process are organized and maintained. This chapter has two purposes: to examine how social practices based on interlocking systems of racism and sexism are maintained in the professionalization of adult education and to suggest strategies that can be used to confront and change these practices. The discussion that follows is part of an ongoing dialogue among the three authors that began in summer 1990 in an adult education graduate class. As an African American female student, a white female student, and a white male professor, we three represented the intersection of different races, genders, and status levels within the academy. Since this dialogue began three years ago, we have attempted to find a perspective from which we can assess how power relations are implemented in the education system and how they can be challenged within that system. These discussions, which have continued on and off over three years, have resulted not only in friendships but in the seeds of this chapter.

## Professionalization and Adult Education

Because there are many definitions of professionalization, it is important for us to specify how we understand this concept in its relation to adult education. For our analysis, we turn to the writings of sociological theorists (Friedson, 1986; Larson, 1977) who show that the modern movements toward

NEW DIRECTIONS FOR ADULT AND CONTINUING EDUCATION, no. 61, Spring 1994  © Jossey-Bass Publishers

professionalization are linked to the rise of industrial capitalism in the mid-1800s. Within this emergent social order, occupations had to create a market for their services and claim special privileges for those who provided these services. Thus, the unit of analysis in this chapter is the occupation of adult education because individuals do not professionalize; occupations do. Although individuals carry out the professionalization process, they always act within institutional and social relations of power, which are givens. Because power, individual and social well-being, and economic rewards are distributed unequally in society along race and gender lines, it is not surprising that the professionalization of adult education reproduces the same inequalities. Our central argument is that both the societal patterns of racism and sexism and any challenges to such patterns are going to be enacted in the professionalization of adult education, because the same people, institutions, and practices construct the patterns in society and the patterns in the occupation.

We must first ask where in the professionalization process these patterns of racism and sexism are manifest. To answer this question, we turn to Larson (1977), who argues that professionalization is the process by which the producers of special services, such as adult education, seek to constitute and control the market for their services. For this professional market to exist, a distinctive commodity must be produced. In contrast to industrial labor, most professions produce intangible goods, and their products are inextricably bound to the persons who produce them. It follows then that the producers, such as adult educators, themselves have to be produced if their products are to be given a distinctive form. In other words, professionals must be adequately trained and socialized so as to provide recognizably distinct services on the professional market. In order to provide such distinct services, the profession must have a recognizably distinct and standardized knowledge base that is taught to new members. All this comes together in higher education, where the production of knowledge and the production of practitioners are united in the same structure. That is, the model of research and training institutionalized by the modern university gives professions the means to control their knowledge base and award credentials certifying that the practitioner possesses this recognizably distinct type of knowledge. The achievement of any profession's socially recognized expertise is therefore necessarily connected to a system of education and credentialing.

On the basis of this analysis, we can say that adult education began to professionalize nearly sixty years ago when degree programs were established in universities. As with any profession, the field's level of professionalization can be assessed by the extent to which its credentials are accepted as necessary to provide a specific type of service. As Larson (1977) explains, marketable expertise is a crucial element in the structural distribution of social power, and professionalization is an attempt to translate one order of scarce resources (special knowledge and skill) into another (social and economic rewards). The direct connection between professionalization and the structure of modern inequality explains why the patterns of discrimination based on race and gender that we see in all other areas of society prevail also in the professionalization of adult education. Professionalization is simply another mechanism by which social power is distributed in society, and all the existing asymmetrical power relationships among different races and between men and women are reproduced (often in complex and subtle ways) through this process. Existing asymmetrical power relations are reproduced in a variety of ways in where adult educators work, in how they organize in professional associations, and in how they are educated and credentialed. Although these three sites (workplace, associations, and higher education) are important in the professionalization process, we have chosen to focus this chapter on the ways in which racism and sexism are manifest in the education and credentialing activities of higher education. We have done so because the evidence is overwhelming that the mechanism for knowledge production and training that occurs in universities is the linchpin of the professionalization process. That is, we have to consider how power relations are being reproduced in the higher education process if we want to understand how power relations (particularly those based on race, gender, or both) are reproduced in the professionalization of the adult education field.

The issue of who has the power to determine what counts as knowledge is extremely important to an understanding of professionalization in adult education. It is clear that, for the most part, the faculty members in higher education settings, particularly at the graduate level, who serve as both teachers and researchers have the power to serve both as producers and as disseminators of knowledge. They produce knowledge in their research pursuits; they also determine what research is "good," what research is to be published and disseminated, and what of the resulting literature is to be included in the curriculum. Minnich (1991, p. 161) notes that, "like power, knowledge depends on the agreement of a significant group of people and establishes itself more firmly as their organization grows. And when that organization is of professionals whose knowledge is itself high in the hierarchy, power takes on the further mantle of authority. In such organizations, it is not at all surprising that the articulated hierarchy of 'kinds' of people is also replicated." Thus, in the next section we discuss three central ways in which racism and sexism are maintained in the professionalization process: the people on adult education faculties, the relationship between who they are and the kind of knowledge that they produce and disseminate through the curriculum, and the ways in which personal interactions are structured.

## Manifestations of Racism and Sexism in Professionalization

As we have argued in the preceding section, the process by which the structured power relations of society are reproduced is the same whether we are considering relations based on race, class, gender, ethnicity, or any other system of structured privilege or oppression. However, these relations are manifest in somewhat different ways in the professionalization process, and so we discuss them separately here. We focus in particular on the ways in which racism and sexism affect African Americans and women.

## Racism in Adult Education

In order to understand how racist practices are evident and propagated in the professionalization of adult education, we must remember that what happens in a higher education setting to a great extent mirrors what is happening in the culture at large. American society is, after all, one of hierarchies, and it is therefore inherently one of divisiveness and power struggles. To be an African American in this country is to be relegated by birth to a position of implicit inferiority. The inequalities that accompany such a position are manifest in all facets of life, particularly in the workplace and in the classroom (Terkel, 1992). African Americans are often stereotyped as less intelligent than the white majority and as lazy, childlike, and violent (Hacker, 1992). They are overrepresented in the service, operative, and laborer occupations (Reskin and Roos, 1990), and they earn fifty-nine cents to every dollar earned by whites (U.S. Bureau of the Census, 1992). These discrepancies persist across educational, professional, and age cohorts (Hacker, 1992; U.S. Bureau of the Census, 1992). Since educational attainment has a positive correlation to professional success, earning potential, and living standards, the inferior education offered to African Americans has been particularly effective in relegating them to the poorer classes (McCarthy, 1990). Although the workplace was not legally separated like the schoolroom, its barriers have been equally formidable. It took the civil rights movement of the 1960s and the laws and enforcement that followed to open the workplace doors to African Americans. Despite the gains that the media have written about, very few substantive changes have occurred (Geschwender and Carroll-Seguin, 1990).

As the authors of Chapter One pointed out, race and gender operate jointly in the lives of African American women. While it is obvious that race is a problem in American society and it is also acknowledged that gender is a major problem, the two are rarely seen as coconspirators. Yet they do combine in a real sense in the lives of black women. Black women are members of two minority groups. In an extensive analysis of the double jeopardy that results, King (1988) explains that the common approach for analyzing the lives of African Americans and women is the race-gender analogy, which subsumes black women as a group and downplays the differences between race and gender. Joseph and Lewis (1981) directly connect the two isms by explaining that the dominant culture thrives while competing minorities struggle for a small piece of the academic and work force pie. They call for cooperation among members of the African American race to fight racism and sexism and for all women to join forces in the struggle against oppression.

**Faculty.** The first way in which racism is manifest in professionalization is in the composition of the faculty of graduate programs. Those who are professors in higher education, those who have been given the power to produce and disseminate knowledge, are in 1993 still almost exclusively white. According to the National Center for Education Statistics (1992), in 1987 91 percent of the full-time faculty at public institutions offering doctoral degrees in all fields were white, and only 1.8 percent were African American. Clearly, those who have the power to create and disseminate knowledge are members of the white hegemonic culture. When we examined the current membership of the Commission of Professors of Adult Education, we found that 178 of the 186 people listed (95 percent) were white. Consequently, those who determine what knowledge is produced, what counts as true knowledge, and what will be included in the curriculum as necessary professional knowledge are still almost exclusively white. Because faculty members are in the business of credentialing adult educators by conferring master's and doctoral degrees, faculty members of the profile just noted act as gatekeepers for the professionalization process. Given the low representation of African Americans among professors in the field, we can safely say that African Americans have not had much power to serve either as producers or as disseminators of knowledge in the field.

While this situation may be changing, it is not changing quickly. At the University of Georgia, 107 graduate students were enrolled in the Department of Adult Education as of this writing. Only eight of this number (approximately 8 percent) are African American. While we do not have access to information about the races represented by the students enrolled in other graduate programs in adult education, we do not have any reason to suspect that other programs are vastly different in this respect. Thus, given the pool of graduate students from which future faculty members will be drawn, it seems likely that the racial composition of the adult education professorate will change only very slowly. The overwhelmingly white and largely male representation on faculties of adult education is not surprising if we recognize that the educational system largely sponsors white males by offering them more classroom attention, more positive reinforcement, a curriculum that offers likely access to higher education and thus potential earning power, and a greater number of role models and mentors from similar backgrounds (*The AAUW Report*, 1992). Another factor influencing the composition of faculty in higher education is the effect of the mentoring process on the placement and recruiting of new faculty. African Americans are not brought into academia in sufficient numbers because they are not adequately mentored by white males—the power brokers of higher education. Moses (1989) cites the lack of mentoring as an important factor barring African American women from the campus network that aids in academic success.

**Curriculum.** Another way in which racism is propagated through higher education becomes evident when we examine the curriculum. What gets taught and what has counted as true knowledge, throughout the entire educational system, has generally represented a white worldview. The works of African Americans are largely excluded from the canon. This strategy keeps the educational process both elitist and homogenous. Freydberg (1993, p. 59) sees this exclusion as the means by which the system safeguards its knowledge and describes the process as a "hall of mirrors . . . which reproduces and authenticates its own legitimacy by drawing upon the same terms it seeks to prove." She explains that such an illusionary process creates a false center and a resulting imperialist infrastructure that uses a divide-and-conquer strategy to retain power. Integration of the curriculum is also cited as a subtle means of reproducing the canon. This method is manifest in several ways. Departments can create special courses whose titles include the words *ethnic* or *black*, or books by and about African Americans can be added to the curriculum. However, such strategies do not change the core curriculum but merely reinforce the identity of the new as other (Farmer, 1993; James, 1993). Farmer (1993, p. 196) disparages the approach for giving "place but not importance." In addition, integration is seen as a way of keeping the canon intact. McCarthy (1990, p. 37) refers to integration as a truce devised to stop disapproval of "assimilationist curriculum models." Given the almost exclusively white composition of adult education faculties, who have historically determined what counts as true knowledge, it is not surprising that curricula in adult education have generally represented a white worldview or that "nonwhite racial groups in the United States are rarely mentioned as the creators of concepts or ideas or as the producers of curricula" (Colin and Preciphs, 1991, p. 65). The fact that the contributions of the African American community are rarely mentioned in the adult education literature suggests that such contributions have not been valued enough to be included in the literature (Colin and Preciphs, 1991). But when African Americans appear in the literature, they are not noted as such. Thus, their contributions are decolorized and assumed to have been contributed by whites.

**Interactions Among Faculty and Students.**  A third way in which racism is maintained in the professionalization process is through the structured interaction among students and faculty. Stereotypes are major supports of racist practices (Reyes and Halcon, 1990), and they are operative both in higher education and in the culture at large. According to Warren (1993, p. 100), "they operate as tacit knowledge that influences conscious and unconscious bias." These convenient ways of classifying the unknown and unfamiliar lead to many of the problems cited by minority students and faculty. African American students say that when they are recognized as exhibiting intelligence and competence, they are seen as unique among African American students, not as the rule. As regards professors, minority faculty report that they are expected to be the caretakers of other minority students and faculty as well as to perform their routine duties of research and teaching, and they are not compensated or credited for the extra work they are thus expected to do. Reyes and Halcon (1990) argue that minority faculty should be credited and recognized for their special contributions. These authors recommend that a value be assigned to "ethnic perspective, cultural knowledge, diversity of ethnic mix in the network of people, and the power to attract other minority students into higher education" (Reyes and Halcon, 1990, p. 82). Moses (1989) and James (1993) acknowledge that minorities are expected to perform the extra duties just described only in reference to other minorities. Yet they are rarely considered competent to perform counseling and support functions for nonminority students or faculty (Moses, 1989). Under the attitude that now prevails, such extra services are not recognized as enhancing the individual's administrative ability.

## Sexism in Adult Education

Power relations in higher and adult education and in the professionalization process parallel those in society and are based on interlocking systems of oppression. It is clear that women have less economic and political power in society than men do. Women's salaries have chronically been lower than those of men who perform the same jobs, and the 1970s and 1980s witnessed the feminization of poverty. Currently, women in the United States earn seventy-one cents to every dollar earned by men (U.S. Bureau of the Census, 1992). One need only examine the composition of the U.S. Congress to see that women have significantly less political power than men in our culture. While women made gains in elections last year, there are still only 6 women (6 percent) out of 100 in the U.S. Senate and 48 (11 percent) out of 435 in the U.S. House of Representatives (Cranford, 1992). In short, women make up more than half the U.S. population, but they still make up less than 10 percent of the U.S. Congress, which underlines the fact that women have far less political and policy-making power than men. Education also plays a major role in the reproduction of power relations based on gender. Males have been sponsored throughout the entire educational system. They receive more attention in the classroom from teachers and peers than women do. Most of the authors whom they read and the researchers who are referenced are from their gender (*The AAUW Report*, 1992). Hence, both conscious and unconscious mechanisms give students the message that the world gives greater value to what the members of more privileged groups—largely white upper-middle-class males—have to say. But our concern in this section is how this validation plays out in the field of adult education.

Faculty. There is evidence that adult education plays a role in the reproduction of power relations based on gender when we examine who serves as producers and disseminators of knowledge in the field, that is, adult education faculty members. Of the 186 current members of the Commission of Professors of Adult Education, 59 (32 percent) were women. This number represents an improvement over higher education circles in general. In 1987, only 25 percent of the full-time teaching faculty at all public institutions in the

United States offering doctoral degrees across all disciplines was female (National Center for Education Statistics, 1992). But given that the vast majority of graduate students in adult education are female, faculties of adult education are not as progressive with regard to gender as they may at first appear to be. At the University of Georgia, 62 percent of the currently enrolled graduate students but only 33 percent of the faculty in adult education are women. While it may be true that increasing numbers of women are being hired for faculty positions in the field, the representation of women on university faculties in adult education is certainly not proportional to their presence in graduate programs or to the number of women receiving doctoral degrees in the field. Indeed, if we can assume that the University of Georgia is representative, it appears that approximately two-thirds of those receiving doctoral degrees in the field are women, while approximately two-thirds of the faculty positions in the field are occupied by men. To explain the discrepancy, one might argue that change is slow and that older male faculty have not yet retired to make their positions available. This is may be true, but there still appears to be a leak in the pipeline.

**Curriculum.** The reproduction of power relations based on gender is also played out in the curriculum required by graduate programs in adult education. Required courses usually include works of such eminent adult educators as Knowles, Freire, and Mezirow, most of whom are white males. While graduate programs in adult education are increasingly offering courses dealing with the interlocking systems of gender and race privilege and oppression, such courses are generally not required, and their status in the field is accordingly marginal. Thus, the overt curriculum of adult education—the courses that all students must take—gives white, upper-middle-class males the greatest credence as producers and disseminators of knowledge in the field. Feminist criticism has generally been lacking from the literature on adult education (Collard and Stalker, 1991). While the situation appears to be changing and recent publications have dealt with feminist issues, fewer women than men have been historically recognized as having contributed to the knowledge base of adult education (Hayes, 1992). Much of the literature dealing with women that does exist tends to portray them in nonauthoritative roles (Collard and Stalker, 1991). In light of the overall lack of attention to feminist theory, the adult education literature and thus the adult education curriculum in higher education have inadvertently reinforced the subordination of women.

**Interactions Among Faculty and Students.** The greater valuing of white male knowledge is also propagated in the hidden curriculum, that is, in what is taught in unconscious ways—through the examples used, in the power dynamics that often emerge in adult education classrooms, and by what often happens in the mentoring process. As Tisdell (1993) has noted, members of the groups used in small-group exercises in adult education classes most often choose white males to be spokespersons, reporters, or leaders despite the fact that the females in such classes very often outnumber the males three to one.

It is not necessarily that the white males in such groups consciously take over or that the females consciously and dutifully acquiesce. Rather, these familiar dynamics are played out everywhere and rooted in the ways in which we are socialized into American culture. After all, most women of every race are used to white males in leadership roles, to the authority of their deeper voices, and to their seemingly more cogent ways of speaking. And white men are generally used to being paid attention to, being deferred to by others, and to speaking out in formal and informal public situations (Renzetti and Curran, 1992). So it is quite natural for white males to be given more attention and more authority by their peers and perhaps by their teachers as well. While we may intellectually believe that women, African Americans, and those otherwise marginalized in our culture are their equals, we have been socialized into a variety of unconscious patterns of relating that generally support white male dominance. These unconscious patterns of relating are generally evident in adult education classrooms (Tisdell, 1993). To the extent to which professors and students fail to critique them as power dynamics emerge in classrooms, they are reinforced in the professionalization process of adult education.

That adult education faculties are still approximately two-thirds male while nearly two-thirds of the doctoral degrees in the field go to women may result in part from the fact that white males are better mentored than women in almost all fields (Grant and Ward, 1992). Internalized patterns of deference may make women less likely to be as proactive as white male peers in asking for help or directly seeking out mentoring. Instead, they may assume that professors are too busy or not interested in helping them (Sadker and Sadker, 1990). Most professors are more likely to mentor those who seek to be mentored. The situation may be complicated by their discomfort with dealing with others, whether the others in question are women or the members of some other marginalized group. Should we ask or expect students from marginalized groups to answer questions about subject matter particularly relevant to their group? Perhaps we worry that such questions will make them uncomfortable. We want to be sensitive, so we are unsure about what to do, and we are therefore uncomfortable ourselves. Thus, students may inadvertently avoid dealing with people from marginalized groups in class and thereby help to reproduce male, white, middle-class dominance. And it is probably more comfortable for professors, who almost all are both white and male, to continue to mentor students who resemble them in those two ways.

## Strategies for Confronting Racism and Sexism

Given the pervasiveness of racism and sexism in society at large, effecting change on these issues in the professionalization of adult education is not a simple matter. Nevertheless, we must confront these problems. Although we have treated racism and sexism separately for the purposes of this chapter, we recognize that similar strategies have been used to co-opt and siphon off power based on racism and sexism. As we undertake this task, we must note that efforts to confront these issues are already taking place in the professionalization process. Most important, both past and present attempts to confront racism and sexism in society through adult education are now being recognized. Cunningham (1989) has documented many such efforts, including the civil rights and women's rights movements, community-based education, adult education in socialism, and workers' education.

**Faculty.** In an effort to sensitize adult educators to the others with whom they must deal, adult education administration can form active liaisons with the women's studies and ethnic studies departments. These departments can direct adult educators to journals and books that can broaden the knowledge base in relation to social issues in education that affect women and African Americans. Not only can faculty from these areas serve on search committees, but they can help to recruit applicants and disseminate hiring information. Networks can also be formed between adult education departments and women's colleges or historically black colleges or universities in the region. Such relationships can be valuable in the recruitment not only of minority and women faculty but also of graduate students.

The recruitment and hiring process is another area in which unconscious values can affect the professionalization of adult education and higher education. Reyes and Halcon (1990) report that the interview process functions differently for minority applicants: Minority candidates are often scrutinized more carefully than other applicants, and they are expected to fit into the traditional white, male academic mold. According to Farmer (1993), search committees explore within their comfort zone and consciously and unconsciously try to replicate themselves. One way of dealing with this issue might be to have faculty in charge of recruitment familiarize themselves with interviewing techniques appropriate for cross-cultural interviews. Personnel offices can provide search committees with a list of questions that may not be asked of women applicants. In addition, a personnel office can provide a list of subject areas or guidelines to follow when interviewing minority and women applicants. While it is important to add minority and women faculty, issues involving retention and tenure are also affected by the unconscious process of stereotyping. James and Farmer (1993) and Reyes and Halcon (1990) both report that minority and women staff often research areas of interest to them as minorities and women. The academy often views such work as less pertinent or essential than work done on and by the majority. Efforts should be made not only to respect the diversity of this research but to encourage and value it as necessary to the good health of the academy.

**Curriculum.** In order to confront racism and sexism in the professionalization of adult education, we must examine how these issues can or are being dealt with in the overt adult education curriculum. Decisions about what to include in the curriculum are political decisions. While the fact that time is limited makes it impossible to include everything that one might like to see in a course, most adult education courses could incorporate at least some required readings, reflection, and discussion related to these issues. If we really want to challenge unequal power relations based on gender and race, it is not enough to make passing comments about these issues in existing classes. Such comments usually get co-opted by the dominant culture. hooks (1989, p. 51) notes that education can be liberating or emancipating only "if it is truly revolutionary because the mechanisms of appropriation within white-supremacist, capitalist patriarchy are able to co-opt with tremendous ease that which merely appears radical or subversive." Thus, if teachers and learners are to begin grappling with the nature of unequal power relations, readings on these issues must be incorporated into the overt curriculum. All university departments must also develop new courses designed specifically to deal directly with power relations based on gender and race, and these courses must become requirements in the adult education core curriculum.

**Interactions Among Faculty and Students.** Adult education instructors who want to challenge structured power relations based on gender and race need to adopt teaching strategies that help to accomplish such a purpose. In a classroom setting, both students and teachers are often trapped by preconceived notions about the other. Racism and sexism can exist in various forms. In reference to the teacher's position, two mistakes often occur. Women and minority students are sometimes assumed to be incapable of producing work of the same quality or in the same quantity as their counterparts. Such assumptions can have the result that, no matter what effort these students put forth, their work is automatically judged as below standard; at the very best, it is scrutinized more carefully than the work of other students. It is unethical to conclude from the fact that one African American student or even several African American students do poorly in a given class that African Americans in general have trouble with its subject matter. Nor do all women think with one brain. Difference in levels of academic ability occur proportionately across the two genders and the several races. Conversely, educators can also err in making allowances for minority and women students and consequently accepting work from them that is inadequate either in quantity or quality. Such bending over backwards in an attempt to accommodate students from disadvantaged groups is another form of racism or sexism. When an educator recognizes that a student's work is not acceptable, it is important not only to inform the student in a constructive way but to attempt to give the student a way of compensating. Prejudging students is inherently unfair to students, and it undermines the educational process. The answers to both dilemmas are the same: Students must be assessed individually and accepted where they are in their academic life, a dialogue must be opened between the teacher and student, and an attempt must be made to address the difficulty and possible discomfort found in educational settings. In attempting to increase our consciousness about power relations in the classroom, we may want to consider such issues as the gender and race of the majority of characters in our illustrative stories and examples, those with whom we have eye contact, and those on whom we rely to carry the discussion (Tisdell, 1993). We might further examine whom we see as leaders of the class and what we may have done to set that person up as a leader. One cannot change what one is not conscious of, and much of the reproduction of power relations happens through unconscious mechanisms.

Finally, while students do not possess the same level of institutional power in the academy that faculty do, they still have a responsibility for examining their educational setting. Despite the barriers that exist, students can reach beyond them to inquire about problems, ask teachers for help, and solicit administrative support for dealing with issues of racism and sexism in both the hidden and the overt curriculum. They can also directly facilitate dealings with racism and sexism by building departmental and university coalitions concerned about these issues. Such coalitions can include students, faculty, and administrators from adult education departments, colleges of education, women's studies programs, and African American studies programs. Given that the dominant discourse in the academy and in society is not concerned with racism or sexism, concerned students and faculty are likely to feel isolated and powerless if they do not form coalitions with others interested in dealing with these issues in the curriculum and in society. Altering the nature of power relations in the academy, in society, and in the professionalization of adult education can happen only if those who are concerned about these issues band together and work proactively for change as an identifiable group or movement.

## Conclusion

We believe that only by challenging the power relations in graduate programs in adult education can we begin to challenge racism and sexism in the professionalization of adult education. We have argued that the power relations in higher education, adult education, and professionalization reflect the power relations of society. Change is difficult and therefore slow, but it is not impossible. We believe that change can be facilitated by adopting some of the strategies outlined here for challenging racism and sexism in graduate programs in adult education. Strategies not mentioned here or that have not yet been formulated may also be useful. We believe that racism and sexism will be better addressed in the professionalization of adult education when traditional models of what counts as true knowledge are called into question, when the adult education curriculum reflects the people and issues that it attempts, and when people with feminist and Afrocentric consciousness are represented on faculties of adult education in greater numbers.

## References

*The AAUW Report: How Schools Shortchange Girls.* Washington, D.C.: AAUW Educational Foundation and National Education Association, 1992.

Colin, S. A. J., III, and Preciphs, T. K. "Perceptual Patterns and the Learning Environment: Confronting White Racism." In R. Hiemstra (ed.), *Creating Environments for Effective Adult Learning.* New Directions for Adult and Continuing Education, no. 50. San Francisco: Jossey-Bass, 1991.

Collard, S., and Stalker, J. "Women's Trouble: Women, Gender and the Learning Environment." In R. Hiemstra (ed.), *Creating Environments for Effective Adult Learning.* New Directions for Adult and Continuing Education, no. 50. San Francisco: Jossey-Bass, 1991.

Cranford, J. "The New Class: More Diverse, Less Lawyerly, Younger." *Congressional Quarterly,* Nov. 7, 1992, pp. 7–12.

Cunningham, P. M. "Making a More Significant Impact on Society." In B. A. Quigley (ed.), *Fulfilling the Promise of Adult and Continuing Education.* New Directions for Continuing Education, no. 44. San Francisco: Jossey-Bass, 1989.

Farmer, R. "Place But Not Importance: The Race for Inclusion in Academe." In J. James and R. Farmer (eds.), *Spirit, Space, and Survival.* New York: Routledge, 1993.

Freydberg, E. H. "American Studies: Melting Pot or Pressure Cooker?" In J. James and R. Farmer (eds.), *Spirit, Space, and Survival.* New York: Routledge, 1993.

Friedson, E. *Professional Powers.* Chicago: University of Chicago Press, 1986.

Geschwender, J. A., and Carroll-Seguin, R. "Exploding the Myth of African American Progress." *Signs,* 1990, *15* (2), 285–299.

Grant, L., and Ward, K. *Mentoring, Gender, and Publication Among Social, Natural, and Physical Scientists: Final Report to the Office of Educational Research and Improvement.* Washington, D.C.: U.S. Department of Education, 1992.

Hacker, A. *Two Nations.* New York: Ballantine Books, 1992.

Hayes, E. "The Impact of Feminism on Adult Education Publications: An Analysis of British and American Journals." *International Journal of Lifelong Education,* 1992, *11* (2), 125–138.

hooks, b. *Talking Back: Thinking Feminist, Thinking Black.* Boston: South End Press, 1989.

James, J. "Teaching Theory, Talking Community." In J. James and R. Farmer (eds.), *Spirit, Space, and Survival.* New York: Routledge, 1993.

James, J., and Farmer, R. (eds.). *Spirit, Space, and Survival.* New York: Routledge, 1993.

Joseph, G. I., and Lewis, J. *Common Differences: Conflicts in Black and White Perspectives.* Boston: South End Press, 1981.

King, D. K. "Multiple Jeopardy, Multiple Consciousness: The Context of a Black Feminist Ideology." *Signs,* 1988, *14* (1), 42–72.

Larson, M. S. *The Rise of Professionalism: A Sociological Analysis.* Berkeley: University of California Press, 1977.

McCarthy, C. "Rethinking Liberal and Radical Perspectives on Radical Inequality in Schooling: Making the Case for Nonsynchrony." In N. M. Hidalgo, C. L. McDowell, and E. V. Siddle (eds.), *Facing Racism in Education.* Cambridge, Mass.: Harvard University Press, 1990.

Minnich, E. K. *Transforming Knowledge.* Philadelphia: Temple University Press, 1990.

Moses, Y. *Black Women in Academe: Issues and Strategies.* Washington, D.C.: Project on the Status and Education of Women, Association of American Colleges, 1989.

National Center for Education Statistics. *Digest of Education Statistics.* Washington, D.C.: U.S. Government Printing Office, 1992.

Renzetti, C., and Curran, D. *Women, Men, and Society.* Needham Heights, Mass.: Allyn & Bacon, 1992.

Reskin, B., and Roos, P. *Job Queues, Gender Queues.* Philadelphia: Temple University Press, 1990.

Reyes, M., and Halcon, J. J. "Racism in Academia: The Old Wolf Revisited." In N. M. Hidalgo, C. L. McDowell, and E. V. Siddle (eds.), *Facing Racism in Education.* Cambridge, Mass.: Harvard University Press, 1990.

Sadker, M., and Sadker, D. "Confronting Sexism in the College Classroom." In S. Gabriel and I. Smithson (eds.), *Gender in the Classroom.* Urbana: University of Illinois Press, 1990.

Terkel, S. *Race: How Blacks and Whites Think and Feel.* New York: New Press, 1992.

Tisdell, E. "Interlocking Systems of Power, Privilege, and Oppression in Adult Higher Education Classes." *Adult Education Quarterly,* 1993, *43* (4), 203–226.

U.S. Bureau of the Census. *Statistical Abstract of the United States: 1992.* Washington, D.C.: U.S. Government Printing Office, 1992.

Warren, N. "Deconstructing, Reconstructing, and Focusing Our Literary Image." In J. James and R. Farmer (eds.), *Spirit, Space, and Survival.* New York: Routledge, 1993.

*JUANITA JOHNSON BAILEY is a doctoral candidate in the Department of Adult Education at the University of Georgia.*

*ELIZABETH J. TISDELL is coordinator of student services for evening classes at the University of Georgia and teaches in the women's studies program.*

*RONALD M. CERVERO is professor of adult education at the University of Georgia.*

*Eliminating racism and sexism requires strategies for personal and professional change.*

# Developing a Personal and Professional Agenda for Change

*Elisabeth Hayes*

> Like a virus, it's hard to beat racism, because by the time you come up with a cure, it's mutated to a "new cure-resistant" form. One shot just won't get it. Racism must be attacked from many angles.
> —J. Yamato (1992, p. 58)

Overcoming racism and sexism is a key concern for society and thus for adult education. As Chapter One suggests, adult education has the potential to be a powerful tool for assisting individuals and institutions to confront racism and sexism, but adult educators must first recognize and eliminate the racism and sexism in their own practice. The authors of the chapters in this sourcebook have pointed out a variety of ways in which racism and sexism are manifest in adult education, and they have described numerous strategies for change.

Given the complexity and enormity of the issues, the barriers to change may seem overwhelming, particularly from the perspective of a single individual. Further, just as perceptions of the problems differ, so do the strategies for change that have been recommended. One thing, perhaps, is consistent: The very enormity of the task demands that we each be involved in the change process.

So how to begin? While there is no formula, the authors and other sources have suggested some key ingredients. In this chapter, I discuss strategies for addressing racism and sexism on two levels: strategies for personal change and strategies for professional change. *Personal change* refers to changing one's own beliefs and actions as an individual educator as well as in other areas of life. *Professional change* refers to educating others about racism and sexism, creating more equitable institutional practices, and confronting biases in and through professional associations. Of course, these two types of change are interrelated, since addressing personal biases is prerequisite for efforts to transform institutions and associations and since these broader transformations will in turn support further individual change.

## Developing a Personal Agenda

The preceding chapters suggest a number of strategies for addressing the biases in one's own practice. I have also drawn from the discussion by Colin and Preciphs (1991) of components that facilitate change in racist perceptions and beliefs. In this section, I discuss six potential elements of an agenda for personal change: awareness and acknowledgement of racism and sexism, commitment to change, understanding and valuing diversity, self-awareness and reflection, affective learning, and developing and evaluating new behaviors. These elements are not linear, discrete steps but rather constant and interrelated aspects of an ongoing and dynamic learning process.

**Awareness and Acknowledgment of Racism and Sexism.** According to Colin and Preciphs (1991), the acknowledgement of racism is an essential first step toward change. Those who are not the objects of racism and sexism are often not aware that they exist, or they perceive the resulting problems as insignificant. While a majority of African Americans see and experience discrimination every day, "only about one white in ten . . . believes that blacks encounter discrimination in getting unskilled jobs or fair wages, and the odds are little better than fifty-fifty that a white person can think of even one type of discrimination from which blacks in their area suffer" (Sigelman and Welch, 1991, p. 165). Similarly, it is likely that many men have no awareness of the prevalence of sexism.

A general awareness of racism and sexism is probably not sufficient to motivate change efforts. Awareness and acknowledgement must extend to the individual's own racist and sexist beliefs and behaviors (Colin and Preciphs, 1991). Obviously, it can be difficult and painful to confront one's own biases. However, once we acknowledge the pervasiveness of racism and sexism in our society, it becomes apparent that we all are likely to hold beliefs and engage in behaviors that are discriminatory.

Acknowledging that racism and sexism exist and increasing our awareness of their manifestations can be accomplished in a variety of ways. An extensive literature describes and analyzes multiple aspects of racism and sexism. One good general introduction, which discusses class issues as well, is Rothenberg's (1992) *Race, Class, and Gender in the United States: An Integrated Study*. Others can be found by consulting the reference lists of the chapters in this volume.

As Amstutz notes in Chapter Four, men's or white people's lack of awareness can be attributed in part to the fact that they have little or no direct experience of racism or sexism. One aspect of increased awareness is an increased ability to understand racism and sexism from the perspective of women and people of color. Films, fiction, drama, autobiography, and poetry are particularly effective tools for heightening one's sensitivity toward the effects of racism and sexism on individual lives and especially of their emotional impact. Friends or colleagues who are people of color or women may be willing to share their experiences of discrimination with you. However, a word of caution is in order. While women or people of color can be good sources of information about sexism and racism, we need to take primary responsibility for educating ourselves. We should not assume that another individual will have the desire or the patience to submit to endless questioning.

Finally, much can be learned from informed observation of everyday situations. Perhaps the most compelling incidents are those that involve people whom one knows personally. I became painfully aware of one type of discrimination while shopping with an African American friend in a large mall. Salespeople ignored her, while I was repeatedly approached and offered assistance. Nothing suggested any difference in our likelihood to make a purchase. I had never been conscious of this type of racism, because I had never had the opportunity to experience it, but now I am quite sensitive to it and to the feelings of exclusion that it created for my friend.

**Commitment to Change.** A second essential aspect of a personal agenda is a commitment to take individual responsibility for changing racist and sexist beliefs and behaviors. All too often, we who are in positions of privilege can believe that oppressed groups have responsibility for pointing out biases and telling us what we should do to address them. Making this commitment can involve an honest examination of one's goals, values, and priorities as an educator and as a person. In Chapter Four, Amstutz suggests that unexamined discrepancies between espoused beliefs and actual behavior help to maintain racism and sexism. If your goals include fostering positive learning experiences for all learners and providing all individuals with access to learning, then you may need to consider whether you can accomplish them without addressing issues of racism and sexism.

**Understanding and Valuing Diversity.** Developing new perspectives on diversity is an integral part of overcoming biases. Colin and Preciphs (1991) suggest that the exchange of information about other cultures and histories is essential if we are to overcome distorted perceptions of various groups of people. Flannery argues in Chapter Two that we must both recognize and value diverse knowledges in order to overcome the biases inherent in allegedly universal truths about adults as learners. Further, both Sheared in Chapter Three and Amstutz in Chapter Four point out the need to acknowledge that people are individuals with unique and complex identities, not members of groups that can be identified and summarized by a single characteristic, such as gender or race.

New perspectives on the diverse experiences, histories, and knowledges of women and people of color can be developed in a variety of ways. Literature, as suggested by Flannery in Chapter Two, can be one source or information about different voices and ways of knowing. In Chapter Five, Colin identifies literature that can offer new insights into African Americans' experiences and roles in adult education. Individuals might undertake the field experiences suggested by Amstutz even without the structure of a formal program. Such experiences do not necessarily require you to go beyond your own community. Volunteer work in a local adult literacy program, a women's counseling center, or other community agency can raise your awareness of the diversity in your own locale. Such experiences do not need to involve formal work or educational programs. For example, individuals might find it easy to undertake the activity of stepping out and stepping in described by Taylor (1993). The activity consists simply of shopping in various ethnic enclaves that are different from your own, getting to know salespeople and other shoppers, and recording events and your feelings and concerns.

These investigations of diversity need to be combined with the task of developing new ways of responding to it, which may be more difficult. Valuing diversity helps us to move beyond hierarchies of difference and "develop new definitions of power and new patterns of relating across difference" (Lourde, 1992, p. 407).

**Self-Awareness and Reflection.** Amstutz identifies self-reflection as a key learning tool for attempts to address issues of racism and sexism; all the other elements described here depend on it. At least two aspects of self-awareness are important. One is one's awareness of one's own "culture" and its values, assumptions, ways of behaving, and ways of knowing. It is important to understand how your beliefs, values, and behaviors are a product of a particular family, socioeconomic class, race, historical moment, and so forth. The second aspect of self-awareness concerns one's own experience of racism and sexism. How has your family dealt with prejudice, racism, sexism, and discrimination? How have these responses affected your own thoughts and behaviors? What examples of racism and sexism have you witnessed or experienced, and what was your emotional, intellectual, and behavioral response? How do your own beliefs and practices reflect racist and sexist assumptions?

Self-awareness and reflection can be stimulated by contact with people whose backgrounds and experiences differ significantly from one's own. As Amstutz suggests, reflection can be promoted through the use of a journal in which one records significant events and one's reactions to readings and experiences. Taylor (1993) recommends that we prepare cultural biographies to clarify how our families are situated in particular cultural and historical identities. Discussion with others can be a particularly valuable tool to stimulate thought and broaden perspectives.

**Affective Learning.** Racism and sexism inevitably generate strong feelings that we may not feel prepared to handle. Distrust of those who are different and dislike or resentment based on stereotypes can be underlying motivators for racist and sexist behaviors. Even when we acknowledge that we have racist and sexist behaviors, emotions can be major obstacles to change. Worrying about our own guilt does not help us to solve the problem. We must become aware of these emotions and their origins and learn to deal with them so that they do not prevent us from acting positively.

Affective learning also can be a valuable means of acquiring increased empathy for those who have experienced racism and sexism (Colin and Preciphs, 1991). To promote such learning, the authors just cited recommend the sharing of significant emotional experiences along with the keeping of journals and open discussion of feelings with others.

**Developing and Evaluating New Behaviors.** Changing racist and sexist behaviors can involve major changes in our teaching methods, curricula, and approaches to program development and leadership. A variety of models can be used as a starting point for such changes. The approach described by Sheared in Chapter Three provides one example of the ways in which instructional strategies could be modified to provide better support for learning by diverse students. The content of instruction must also be addressed in the process of overcoming biases. Examples of different phases of curricular transformation may be useful in guiding and evaluating your own change efforts. The model described by Marchesani and Adams (1992) includes five phases of curriculum revision—the exclusive curriculum, the exceptional outsider, understanding the outsider, getting inside the outsider, and the transformed curriculum. Each phase has a different orientation toward traditionally excluded groups. It is probably most realistic to take a gradual, developmental approach to such changes and to build on increased awareness and skills. Other educators have reported that considerable time and reflection are the necessary foundation for new curricular and instructional approaches that are more inclusive of women and minorities (Tetrault, 1985).

Dealing with subtle biases, such as those reflected in informal interactions or use of language, may pose an even greater challenge. In Chapter Six, Bailey, Tisdell, and Cervero point out the role that this hidden curriculum plays in the perpetuation of racist and sexist biases. Overcoming such biases depends first on becoming more aware of them. You can raise your awareness by reading such publications as *The Classroom Climate: A Chilly One for Women?* (Hall, 1982), which provides one good overview of specific teacher behaviors and language that can be discriminatory. It offers helpful suggestions for addressing these biases in your own teaching and in other interactions with students. Given the complexity of classroom dynamics, teachers are often not able to assess their own behaviors with any accuracy. Asking a colleague or student to observe your interactions in the classroom is a valuable way of determining whether you are inadvertently treating women or minority students differently. If biases are identified, observations and feedback are important as you attempt to change your behavior. You also might consider your behavior in other situations, such as meetings or conferences. With whom do you interact at conferences and meetings? Do your interactions with men and women, white people and people of color differ in any way? Who receives more of your attention in staff meetings? Do you respond differently to the comments of men or women, white people or people of color?

## Developing a Professional Agenda

When discussing a professional agenda, I shift the focus to how we can work with others to create broader changes, through our teaching, in our institutional practices, and in our professional associations. This work involves not only educating ourselves and eliminating biases from our own practice but also educating others about racism and sexism and helping them to recognize racism and sexism in their own actions and develop strategies that can overcome them.

Antiracist and feminist educators have developed ideas and strategies that can serve as a starting point for such efforts. One guiding framework can be found in the discussion of antiracist education by Thomas (1984). As Das Gupta (1993) suggests, although Thomas's approach focuses on racism, its principles can also be applied to sexism.

Thomas (1984) identifies not only similarities but also some important differences between antiracist education and traditional approaches to multiculturalism. Multicultural education has tended to emphasize the sharing of information about different cultures and the fostering of appreciation for them as ways of increasing social equity. In contrast, antiracist education focuses on the nature and origins of unequal power relationships among different groups of people and on the ways in which racist beliefs and actions justify these inequities. Antiracist education makes racism and sexism its objects of study, and it acknowledges and confronts them directly. We cannot assume that they will disappear if we simply develop more information about diversity or increase the value that we place on it. In fact, Thomas (1984) argues that existing power inequities limit the aspects of different cultures that we can express, understand, and value.

The article by Thomas (1984) describes five key principles of antiracist education. First, it exposes racist beliefs and stereotypes and examines critically the ways in which the media, the family, and other social institutions promulgate them. Second, it treats culture as complex and dynamic. It emphasizes the significance of multiple factors, such as gender, social class, and age, in people's lives and rejects simplified and romanticized generalizations about customs or life-styles. It emphasizes understanding how people actively create culture and in particular on how oppression has affected and challenged them. Third, it recognizes the role of the economy and the educational system in fostering inequities. One of its goals is to help learners understand and develop skills for challenging these broader factors that contribute to divisiveness and conflicts among groups of people. Fourth, it believes that both the oppressed and the oppressors must be engaged in overcoming inequities. It supports learners in their efforts to challenge racism in their daily lives. It acknowledges that resistance is likely, and it develops strategies for dealing with it. Fifth, it assumes that collective action is necessary to address institutionalized racism. In particular, educators need to work together to challenge the institutional factors that limit their ability to discuss and develop strategies to resist racism. Ultimately, Thomas (1984, p. 24) writes, "antiracist education is also political education, for it examines critically those explanations and practices which misinform and oppress people. It challenges current power relations by attempting to create effective ways of working together and by educating, equipping, and mobilizing people—both children and adults—to recognize injustice and change it."

These principles can become the foundation for specific antiracist, feminist teaching strategies (Das Gupta, 1993) as well as for efforts to challenge racism and sexism in institutions and in professional organizations.

**Teaching.** In Chapter Six, Bailey, Tisdell, and Cervero argue that, if we are to counter racism and sexism effectively, we must deal with them directly in the classroom as part of the overt curriculum. Further, in an antiracist, feminist approach, they become central issues that are integrated throughout the curriculum, not separate or merely additional topics. Not only should the contributions and perspectives of women and people of color be included throughout the curriculum, "the process of learning should lead students to consider as a matter of course what biases and assumptions are reflected in the treatment of a topic, in terms of the questions that are asked, the range of perspectives brought to bear, the conclusions drawn, and the questions which remain" (Tator, 1987–1988, p. 8).

The pervasiveness of racism and sexism suggests that this approach can be applied to any educational situation, with any topic, and with any student population. Tator (1987–1988) describes its application in a wide range of academic subjects, including math, science, and geography, as well as in the more typical areas of literature and history. For example, she describes a staff development workshop for math teachers in which it was suggested that data on discrimination complaints to the Ontario Human Rights Commission could be used in teaching statistics and graphs. This approach could easily be applied to other topics in adult education programs. For example, continuing education programs for health professionals could encourage participants to examine potential racist or sexist biases in new and current medical treatments. They could consider such issues as whether the health concerns of women or people of color receive less attention than those of white men or whether the treatments recommended are based on studies of biased samples. Shor's (1980) description of the way in which sexism was addressed in a writing class for working-class adults could be used to develop a process that could help learners to identify and question their own stereotypes.

One important aspect of the learning experience should be helping learners to develop skills enabling them to take action against racism and sexism.

At least three different kinds of skills or abilities are important: the ability to identify biases in current knowledge and practices, the skills needed for confronting racism and sexism actively, and the skills needed for collective action, in particular to challenge racism and sexism on an institutional and societal level. One way of helping learners to deal with confrontation is to provide a model in your own actions as an educator. One essential aspect of antiracist, feminist teaching is actively to confront any sexism and racism that appears in classroom situations. It is one thing to discuss racism and sexism as problems "out there" and quite another to deal with them as manifest in the dynamics of your classroom. You must be prepared both to subject your own actions and statements to scrutiny and to scrutinize the actions and statements of your students. Such actions can require real courage on the part of teacher and learners as well as strategies for constructive confrontation. Weinstein and Obear (1992) point out that dealing with racism and sexism in teaching situations puts both teacher and learner in emotionally charged and risky positions. They identify a variety of fears that constrain teachers when faced with bias issues. The fears include the possibility of confronting their own biases, doubts about their competency in relation to the issues, their need for the approval of their students, concerns about handling intense emotions, and fear of losing control. Increased self-understanding and strategies for handling potentially difficult situations can reduce all the fears just identified. It is also important to acknowledge that dealing with bias issues always creates discomfort for everyone involved and that such discomfort may be a prerequisite for change.

In helping learners to develop collective action skills, sensitivity to differences in power and perspective among individuals may be critical. Ellsworth (1989) observes that such differences affect the extent to which learners feel safe expressing their opinions about such issues as racism and sexism, to which they can agree on appropriate action, and to which they will be able to work together. She suggests that activities designed to foster trust and personal commitment among learners be used as a starting point for collaborative work. By addressing differences of power and perspective openly in the classroom, learners can gain an awareness and ability to deal with these issues in change-oriented groups outside the classroom.

**Institutional Practices.** Challenging racism and sexism on an institutional level is essential to promote a supportive environment for antiracist and feminist teaching as well as increased equity in the practice of adult education. The belief of individuals that they do not have the power or the responsibility for initiating change can itself be a barrier to institutional change. However, Bogart (1989) reviewed the histories of institutions that have been successful in responding to the needs of women and minorities and concluded that a few key individuals typically serve as catalysts for institutional change. Further, as Pearson, Shavilik, and Touchton (1989, p. 365) argue, while it may be easier for individuals in leadership positions, "if you have the skills of persuasion, the commitment to change, and the ability to build and use networks, you can initiate change."

The authors of the chapters in this sourcebook have described various strategies for overcoming racism and sexism on an institutional level, including changes in student recruitment and admissions policies, faculty hiring practices, staff development strategies, and curricular revisions. While other examples specific to adult education may be hard to find, there are many relevant examples of strategies used in higher education for overcoming institutional racism and sexism and fostering institutional environments that support diversity in a broad sense. In this section, I summarize some key aspects of successful institutional change that might be applied to adult education.

*Groups and Networks as Change Agents.* While individuals are instrumental in initiating change, change cannot be accomplished without group efforts. Collective efforts are needed to identify problems, raise awareness, generate support, and develop and implement change strategies. Hunt, Bell, Wei, and Ingle (1992) describe the roles of varied formal committees at several institutions in efforts to promote widespread institutional changes. Informal networks have also been effective in these roles (Bogart, 1989).

*Clarification of Goals and Values.* Another theme is the need to clarify the goals for institutional change and the values that inform these goals. It is almost guaranteed that different people will have differing understandings of key issues and desirable changes. For example, some may feel that increasing the participation of women and people of color as staff and learners in existing programs may be the key to eliminating racism and sexism, while others may believe that a major transformation of institutional programs is the answer. While such differences may seem to create insurmountable barriers to action, groups have been able to reach consensus by focusing initially on overarching ideals rather than on specific ways of achieving these ideals (Hunt, Bell, Wei, and Ingle, 1992). A pluralistic change strategy can be developed that allows for different approaches if they serve common ends.

*Long-Term Professional Development.* Formal and informal professional development programs for teachers, staff, and administrators have been one major component of change at most institutions. As Amstutz states in Chapter Four, sporadic, one-time workshops do not accomplish meaningful professional development. Successful programs have involved participants for extended periods of time in varied learning opportunities. Moreover, ongoing support has been critical as teachers develop new teaching strategies and curricula or as program planners develop new ways of working with diverse groups.

*Collaboration with Community Groups.* Collaboration with groups outside the institution can be valuable at all stages and in all aspects of the change process, including planning, professional development, student and staff recruitment, and curricular change. For example, LaBare and Lang (1992) describe a variety of community collaborations that St. Norbert College in Wisconsin used to diversify its student body, faculty, and curricula. The college formed an initial partnership with the Menominee tribe that led to off-campus courses in the Native American community, workshops for faculty, student scholarships, and summer precollege programs. The institution subsequently obtained a major grant to work in partnership with a historically black college, a tribal community college, and a socially diverse urban Chicago college. What seems to be critical in these partnerships is the collaborative nature of the relationships. Rather than simply recruiting "stars" from the minority community, the institution engages its partners in a process of mutual development and growth.

*Integration with Overall Mission.* Significant and lasting institutional change appears to depend on making equity an integral part of the overall institutional mission. To make equity happen, it needs to become a priority throughout the institution, not primarily a concern of a special office or program (Hunt, Bell, Wei, and Ingle, 1992). For equity to become a priority, the institution needs a system that rewards teachers and staff for participating in change efforts, and the commitment of institutional leaders and policy-making groups is essential.

Finally, the reader needs to keep in mind that every institution has its own distinctive culture and that change strategies must be designed to work within to that culture (Pearson, Shavilik, and Touchton, 1989). Rather than searching for one institutional model, it is probably most effective to draw ideas from the experience of others while developing strategies specific to your own setting.

**Professional Associations.** An agenda for challenging racism and sexism in adult education should not overlook the professional associations. Like individuals and institutions, our professional groups perpetuate racist and sexist practices and policies. Biases may be found in formal practices, such as appointment of officers, criteria for the selection of conference topics and presenters, or membership requirements. Informal practices, such as networking, interactions at meetings, and mentoring of new members, can also be biased. A variety of strategies may be necessary to identify and overcome such biases. For example, the American Educational Research Association has created permanent committees on the role and status of women and minorities in educational research and development. There are also a number of special-interest groups focusing on the educational needs of women and people of color. The association monitors and publishes annual reports on the participation of women and people of color as association officers, editorial board members, and authors in their association publications. It has also monitored the involvement of women as speakers at its annual conferences. A minority dissertation fellowship program provides association support for new minority educational researchers.

Overcoming racism and sexism in adult education more broadly might become a priority in the mission of our professional associations. Such a development could lead to the sponsoring of publications, conferences, and other activities that educate the profession about racism and sexism. Ross (1989) identifies data collection, dissemination of effective models, enhancement of graduate and professional training, an expanded research agenda, and policy development as necessary to make adult education more responsive to cultur-ally diverse adults. All these activities might become part of our professional associations' broader agenda for change.

## Dealing with Conflict

Conflict is a key issue in challenging racism and sexism in all areas—your own teaching, your institution, and the professional groups to which you belong. Conflict can result from divergent perspectives on the problems of racism and sexism and on the strategies that are appropriate for dealing with them. Indeed, conflict may be unavoidable in groups that include women and men, white people and people of color, whose lived experiences of oppression are very dif-ferent. The challenge is to acknowledge conflict yet not allow it to create insur-mountable barriers to collective action: "What is important is not to deny conflict, but to recognize that in a society like the United States, which is so deeply split by gender, race, and class, conflict is inevitable and only reflects social and political realities. But recognition of conflict, oppression, and power does not mean their acceptance. It means making them conscious so they can be transformed" (Weiler, 1988, pp. 144–145). Conflict can be used to stimu-late growth and transformation of individual perspectives as well as innovative strategies for change. For example, Hunt, Bell, Wei, and Ingle (1992) describe how conflict among faculty with different orientations to multiculturalism at one institution led to the creation of a new curriculum that drew on the strengths of both orientations. The conflict was resolved only when individu-als became willing to listen to each others' views and identify commonalities while valuing the unique contribution that each view could make to a more inclusive perspective.

## Conclusion

Ultimately, our individual efforts to challenge racism and sexism can contribute to changes on a societal level. A final element of this change is developing new visions of community, such as the expanding community proposed by Greene (1993), that are based on concrete engagements with others, through which we affirm and value our diversity as well as our commonalities. We may also need new visions of our roles and responsibilities as adult educators in foster-ing social transformation that draw on our neglected tradition of adult educa-tion for social change (Cunningham, 1989). Challenging racism and sexism means challenging ourselves as well as others to take action against injustices that affect all of us. As hooks (1989, p. 26) writes, it also means a challenge to love: "Love can be and is an important source of empowerment when we struggle to confront issues of sex, race, and class. Working together to identify and face our differences—to face the ways we dominate and are dominated—to change our actions, we need a mediating force that can sustain us so that we are not broken in the process, so that we do not despair. . . . As we work to be loving, to create a culture that celebrates life, that makes love possible, we move against dehumanization, against domination."

## References

Bogart, K. "Toward Equity in Academe: An Overview of Strategies for Action." In C. S. Pearson, D. L. Shavilik, and J. G. Touchton (eds.), *Educating the Majority: Women Challenge Tradition in Higher Education*. New York: American Council on Education and Macmillan, 1989.

Colin, S.A.J., III, and Preciphs, T. K. "Perceptual Patterns and the Learning Environment: Confronting White Racism." In R. Hiemstra (ed.), *Creating Environments for Effective Adult Learning*. New Directions for Adult and Continuing Education, no. 50. San Francisco: Jossey-Bass, 1991.

Cunningham, P. "Making a More Significant Impact on Society." In B. A. Quigley (ed.), *Fulfilling the Promise of Adult and Continuing Education*. New Directions for Continuing Education, no. 44. San Francisco: Jossey-Bass, 1989.

Das Gupta, T. "Towards an Antiracist, Feminist Teaching Method." *New Horizons in Adult Education*, 1993, 7 (1), 33–51.

Ellsworth, E. "Why Doesn't This Feel Empowering? Working Through the Repressive Myths of Critical Pedagogy." *Harvard Educational Review*, 1989, 59 (3), 297–323.

Greene, M. "The Passions of Pluralism: Multiculturalism and the Expanding Community." *Educational Researcher*, 1993, 22 (1), 13–18.

Hall, R. *The Classroom Climate: A Chilly One for Women?* Washington, D.C.: Project on the Status and Education of Women, 1982.

hooks, b. *Talking Back: Thinking Feminist, Thinking Black*. Boston, Mass.: South End Press, 1989.

Hunt, J. A., Bell, L. A., Wei, W., and Ingle, G. "Monoculturalism to Multiculturalism: Lessons from Three Public Universities." In M. Adams (ed.), *Promoting Diversity in College Classrooms: Innovative Responses for the Curriculum, Faculty, and Institutions*. New Directions for Teaching and Learning, no. 52. San Francisco: Jossey-Bass, 1992.

LaBare, M. J., and Lang, S. G. "Institutional Transformation for Multicultural Education: Bloomfield College and St. Norbert College." In M. Adams (ed.), *Promoting Diversity in College Classrooms: Innovative Responses for the Curriculum, Faculty, and Institutions*. New Directions for Teaching and Learning, no. 52. San Francisco: Jossey-Bass, 1992.

Lourde, A. "Age, Race, Class, and Sex: Women Redefining Difference." In P. Rothenberg (ed.), *Race, Class, and Gender in the United States: An Integrated Study*. New York: St. Martin's Press, 1992.

Marchesani, L. S., and Adams, M. "Dynamics of Diversity in the Teaching-Learning Process: A Faculty Development Model for Analysis and Action." In M. Adams (ed.), *Promoting Diversity in College Classrooms: Innovative Responses for the Curriculum, Faculty, and Institutions*. New Directions for Teaching and Learning, no. 52. San Francisco: Jossey-Bass, 1992.

Pearson, C. S., Shavilik, D. L., and Touchton, J. G. (eds.). *Educating the Majority: Women Challenge Tradition in Higher Education*. New York: American Council on Education and Macmillan, 1989.

Ross, J. M. "Reaching and Involving Culturally Diverse Groups." In B. A. Quigley (ed.), *Fulfilling the Promise of Adult and Continuing Education*. New Directions for Continuing Education, no. 44. San Francisco: Jossey-Bass, 1989.

Rothenberg, P. (ed.) *Race, Class, and Gender in the United States: An Integrated Study*. New York: St. Martin's Press, 1992.

Shor, I. *Critical Teaching and Everyday Life*. Boston, Mass.: South End Press, 1980.

Sigelman, L., and Welch, S. *Black Americans' Views of Racial Inequality: The Dream Deferred*. New York: Cambridge University Press, 1991.

Tator, C. "Antiracist Education." *Currents: Readings in Race Relations*, 1987–1988, 4 (4), 8–11.

Taylor, E. *Adult Multicultural Education: A Course and Resource Guide.* Unpublished manuscript. Athens: University of Georgia, 1993.

Tetrault, M. K. "Feminist Phase Theory: An Experience-Driven Evaluation Model." *Journal of Higher Education*, 1985, 56 (4), 363–384.

Thomas, B. "Principles of Antiracist Education." *Currents: Readings in Race Relations*, 1984, 2 (3), 20–24.

Weiler, K. *Women Teaching for Change.* South Hadley, Mass.: Bergin and Garvey, 1988.

Weinstein, G., and Obear, K. "Bias Issues in the Classroom: Encounters with the Teaching Self." In M. Adams (ed.), *Promoting Diversity in College Classrooms: Innovative Responses for the Curriculum, Faculty, and Institutions.* New Directions for Teaching and Learning, no. 52. San Francisco: Jossey-Bass, 1992.

Yamato, J. "Something About the Subject Makes It Hard to Name." In P. Rothenberg (ed.), *Race, Class, and Gender in the United States: An Integrated Study.* New York: St. Martin's Press, 1992.

*ELISABETH HAYES is associate professor of continuing and vocational education at the University of Wisconsin–Madison.*

# INDEX

Academic skill proficiency, 10
Accountability, 34
Adams, M., 81
Adelman, C., 11
Adorno, T., 57
Adult Continuing Education Black Graduate Students Association, 58
Adult development theories: motivational theory (Maslow), 20–21; stages of man (Erikson), 19
*Adult Education Quarterly,* 55
Adult learning theory, 17, 19, 21–22; graduate courses in, 58; in search for universal truth, 20
Adults as learners, universal theories for understanding, 20–22
Affective domain experiences, 47
Affective learning, 80–81
Affiliation, need for, 21
Affirmative action, 55
African Ameripeans, rationale for term, 3n
African Communities League, 56
Africentric epistemology, 32
Africentric feminist perspective, 29
Africentrism, rationale for term, 3n
American Association for Adult Education, 57
American Educational Research Association, 86
Amstutz, Donna, 2, 39, 78, 79, 80, 85
Andragogy, 21
Antiracist education, 82–83, 84
Aptheker, B., 36
Assimilationist curriculum models, 68
Autonomy, 21

Bailey, J. J.n, 3, 63, 81, 83
Bailey, S. M., 10, 13, 14
Barkley-Brown, E., 28, 31
Barnett, R. C., 19
Baruch, G. K., 19
Belenky, M., 33
Belief systems, 6
Bell, L. A., 85, 86, 87
Benokraitis, N. V., 7, 12, 14
Bias: in curriculum, 13, 53, 81; effect of, on knowledge building, 22; organizational policies and, 14; in professional

associations, 86; recognizing, 43, 84; role of, in change, 78; stereotypes and, 68; in students, 34
Biological differences, 6
*Black Issues in Higher Education,* 59
*Black Scholar,* 59
Bogart, K., 84, 85
Both/or orientation, 30, 32
Briscoe, D. B., 22, 24
Brockett, R. G., 19
Brookfield, S. D., 49

Caliver, A., 57
Call-and-response discourse, 35–36
Candy, P. C., 21
Cannon, L., 11, 13
Carroll-Seguin, R., 66
Cassara, B. B., 22
Cervero, R., 3, 63, 81, 83
Chafe, W., 6
Circular reasoning, 18–19
Civil rights movement, 7, 66
Clark, M. C., 22
*Classroom Climate: A Chilly One for Women?, The,* 81
Clinchy, B., 33
Cognitive domain experiences, 47
Colin, A.J.S., III, 2, 3n, 5, 6, 28, 46, 53, 54, 55, 56, 57, 58, 59, 60, 68, 78, 79, 80, 81
Collard, S., 18, 70
Collective action skills, 84
Collins, P. H., 7, 29, 30, 32, 33
Commission of Professors of Adult Education (CPAE), 40, 54, 58, 67, 69
Community, new visions of, 87
Community groups, collaboration with, 85–86
Community Internship Program, 48
Conflict, 87
Continuing professional education, 39, 83
Cranford, J., 69
Critical self-reflection, 46, 49
Cross, W. E., 58
Cross-cultural experiences, 48
Cross-cultural job interviews, 72
Cultural identity, 40
Culture, defined, 40

# ORDERING INFORMATION

NEW DIRECTIONS FOR ADULT AND CONTINUING EDUCATION is a series of paperback books that explores issues of common interest to instructors, administrators, counselors, and policy makers in a broad range of adult and continuing education settings—such as colleges and universities, extension programs, businesses, the military, prisons, libraries, and museums. Books in the series are published quarterly in Spring, Summer, Fall, and Winter and are available for purchase by subscription and individually.

SUBSCRIPTIONS for 1994 cost $47.00 for individuals (a savings of 25 percent over single-copy prices) and $62.00 for institutions, agencies, and libraries. Please do not send institutional checks for personal subscriptions. Standing orders are accepted.

SINGLE COPIES cost $15.95 when payment accompanies order. (California, New Jersey, New York, and Washington, D.C., residents please include appropriate sales tax.) Billed orders will be charged postage and handling.

DISCOUNTS FOR QUANTITY ORDERS are available. Please write to the address below for information.

ALL ORDERS must include either the name of an individual or an official purchase order number. Please submit your order as follows:
   *Subscriptions:* specify series and year subscription is to begin
   *Single copies:* include individual title code (such as ACE 59)

MAIL ALL ORDERS TO:
   Jossey-Bass Publishers
   350 Sansome Street
   San Francisco, California 94104-1342

FOR SINGLE-COPY SALES OUTSIDE OF THE UNITED STATES, CONTACT:
   Maxwell Macmillan International Publishing Group
   866 Third Avenue
   New York, New York 10022-6221

FOR SUBSCRIPTION SALES OUTSIDE OF THE UNITED STATES, contact any international subscription agency or Jossey-Bass directly.

OTHER TITLES AVAILABLE IN THE
NEW DIRECTIONS FOR ADULT AND CONTINUING EDUCATION SERIES
Ralph G. Brockett, Editor-in-Chief
Alan B. Knox, Consulting Editor